# Down the Rabbit Hole and Back Again

## Tales of Life's Challenges, Resilience and the Power of Family Love

## Breda McAlinden

Ultimate World Publishing
Diamond Creek,
Victoria Australia 3089
www.writeabook.com.au

# Acknowledgements

This book was conceived and written on the land of the Kaurna People. We acknowledge and respect their spiritual relationship with their land and country. We acknowledge the Kaurna people as the custodians of the Adelaide region. Their cultural and heritage beliefs are important throughout time.

# Contents

# Introduction

For a long time, I have wanted to write a story – the story of my own life. There are several reasons for this, one of which is knowing that many others have struggled just like I did. The belief that I can do this came alive when my sister recently said to me, 'I do not know anyone in my life who has been through as much as you have.' I dislike labels like victim or survivor. However, I did develop a sense of self-preservation and grew some armour of protection around me to manage the interaction between my inner world and outer world. I can relate a life that is unique in many ways, and I often wonder how different I would have been if I had not experienced the unexpected events that entered my life seemingly out of nowhere. Perhaps one day, the origins of these experiences sent from the dark side of the moon can be understood.

Drafting my story has provided a space where I have explored my world, a world where most people have never been. For those who have, I invite you to join me on this healing journey together.

# Down the Rabbit Hole and Back Again

I would say that I have been down the rabbit hole and back up again more than a few times in my life.

I chose this title for my book, not only because I believe it is true, but also because when we were kids, there was an old gentleman who lived close to us. He was a bandmaster and came to our home to teach us music. As a mischievous child, I would play tricks by standing behind him and placing items on his head. He would always tell me that he had special powers and would turn me into a rabbit if I was not good. I actually believed him, and I was so scared that he would do this to me!

# Dedication

This book is dedicated to my twin kidney sister Philomena, who donated her perfectly matched kidney to me when we were 22 and 19 years old. It was a gift like no other: the gift of life.

I would also like to thank my family, Mum, and Dad, for being with me in spirit throughout the process of drafting my story. To my sisters Rosemary, Philomena, Trish, and our brother Philip, the unconditional love, warmth, and protection I received from all of you supplied a solid foundation to always return to, to refill my bucket, and to keep my resilience alive and well.

To my husband, partner, and father of our children, Cathal, who is now deceased: my love is with you every day, and I thank you for the times you have come to console me in my dreams. To our sons Jordan and Dion and our grandson Iggy: I am forever grateful for the love we share as a family. I am grateful for the gifts I have been given, including the ability to complete this memoir, and I look forward to more writing in the future.

The following symbol represents a heart surrounded by two kidneys on its outer layer, underscoring the immense significance of the decision to selflessly part with one of these precious organs. This powerful emblem serves to symbolise the extraordinary virtues of selflessness and courage, showcasing the remarkable self-sacrifice involved in kidney donation.

**Symbol of selflessness and courage.**

# Chapter 1

# Tales of Emerald Fields

I was born into a strong and proud Irish family, in County Meath. I have four siblings – three sisters and one brother – and I was the fourth girl in the family, with my baby brother being the youngest. Our family has been farming for many generations. The name of our townland is 'Edengora', and just the mention of this name conjures up so many fond memories of living and growing up in this community.

# Down the Rabbit Hole and Back Again

**Our homestead in Edengora.**

The homestead in Edengora is captured in this magical photo taken by my beloved husband, Cathal, who passed away in December 2020. May he rest in peace.

It comes as no surprise that our family roots are firmly planted in the land of the beautiful Emerald Isle. I am so grateful that I grew up in such a rich culture with the strength of family and community surrounding us. My dad was one of ten children, and my mum was one of four. Growing up our lives were filled with family and community.

# Tales of Emerald Fields

The connection to family and community was familiar and special. We had grandparents, aunts, uncles and at least sixty first cousins. Our farm primarily involved dairy and crops during my childhood. I remember the harvesting season when all the farmers would gather on each other's farms to help. There was little machinery back then, and much of the work was manual labour. There was great camaraderie and fun when all the farmers would come together to work. I distinctly remember when it was our turn to host the others; our kitchen would be bustling. The working men would have a hot lunch between 12 pm and 1 pm, complete with dessert. In the afternoon, we would prepare a picnic of sandwiches and tea in glass bottles, and us kids would take it to wherever the men were working. We would find a shady spot, set up the picnic, and the men would join us. We always packed extra sandwiches for ourselves, and the tea in glass bottles was the absolute best tea I have ever tasted.

**Mum and Dad with their first-born Rosemary 1958.**

# Down the Rabbit Hole and Back Again

**By 1965 there were five of us children.
From left: Rosemary, Trish, Philomena,
Breda, and Philip (front).**

Dad was known in the community to be a great herder in looking after cows and sheep when they are about to give birth. The local farmers would come in search for our dad to help if they were running into any difficulties. At times people would even call in the dead of night and Dad would be dressed and out the door in a jiffy, always ready to help.

My dad was a gentle soul, and I was attached to him in a spiritual and nurturing way. I felt safe and loved by my parents. My mum was well grounded, a worker, who could do almost anything around the home. Mum would cook, bake, and renovate the home at regular intervals. When summer evenings were long and bright, we would be playing outside around the home and farm long into the night. Mum and Dad showed us true kindness and unconditional love and taught us unbelievably valuable lessons in life, for example, hard work never killed anyone, kindness starts at home, always say your prayers.

We always had supper together as a family, usually around 9 pm when all the jobs were done for the day and Dad had removed his welly boots and sat to rest for the evening. We would all sit around our large square table together and Mum would cook us up a supper of fried egg, bacon, traditional Irish sausages, and homemade brown bread.

# Chapter 2

# Enchanting Ireland – Its Natural and Cultural Beauty

With its rugged cliffs plunging into the wild Atlantic, mist-laden mountains, and emerald landscapes stretching as far as the eye can see, Ireland truly is a paradise for nature lovers. The landscape is characterised by rolling hills and is dotted with fields and meadows creating a lush, green countryside. From its atmospheric towns to fairytale castles and remote islands, Ireland is the land where beauty is matched by variety.

# Down the Rabbit Hole and Back Again

The culture in Ireland is vibrant and has a deep-rooted history. The country is famous for its traditional music, dance, literature, and its Gaelic language that is still spoken in some rural parts of Ireland. Traditional Irish dancing, with its rhythmic footwork, is now popular worldwide. The Irish people are known for their warmth, friendliness and hospitality. Ireland has a rich literary heritage, with many famous writers and poets hailing from the country. Renowned authors such as James Joyce, Oscar Wilde, WB Yeats and Samuel Beckett have played significant roles in shaping modern literature.

Ireland's natural beauty, cultural heritage and warm hospitality make it a popular destination for tourists from around the world. Visitors can explore its stunning landscapes, immerse themselves in traditional music and dance, learn about its fascinating history and experience the unique charm of the Emerald Isle.

## Irish folklore, mythology and heritage sites

Our parents and grandparents would share traditional stories about folklore with us children. There were stories of fairy lore and cures associated with holy wells. Visiting holy wells was one of our family's favourite outings on a Sunday afternoon. We would throw a coin into the holy well, say a prayer, and ask for some favour to be granted.

Fairies feature greatly in the folklore with references to fairy forts, fairy rings, fairy paths and fairy trees. As kids we were fascinated by the possibility that we may have fairies and leprechauns in our garden. The origin of leprechauns – small, mischievous creatures with special powers to grant wishes who protected their hidden pots of gold in the fields – can be traced back to ancient Irish mythology. Famous Irish writers like WB Yeats and Lady Gregory

# Enchanting Ireland – Its Natural and Cultural Beauty

played a significant role in popularising Irish folklore including tales of leprechauns. The creation of folk stories about leprechauns reflects the rich storytelling tradition and cultural heritage of Ireland.

Ireland has many heritage sites throughout the country. Our own County Meath is home to one of the most famous heritage sites, The Boyne Valley, Newgrange. This site dates back to 3,200 BCE, making it older than Stonehenge and the Egyptian pyramids. Newgrange consists of a large circular mound, around 85 metres in diameter and 13.5 metres high and covers an area of about one acre. The mound is made of earth and stones and is surrounded by a retaining wall of white quartz. The tomb's entrance is aligned with the rising sun on the winter solstice, December 21st, allowing sunlight to penetrate through to the inner chamber illuminating it for about 17 minutes. This phenomenon demonstrates the advanced astronomical knowledge and architectural skills of the Neolithic people who built it.

The passage into the chamber is approximately 19 metres long and leads to a central chamber with three smaller chambers branching off from it. The main chamber contains a basin stone with intricate carvings, and the walls of the chambers are adorned with ancient megalithic spirals.

A designated World Heritage Site, and classified as an Ancient Temple, Newgrange is a place of astrological, spiritual, religious and ceremonial importance. It is believed to have served as a burial site for a community of people who practised complex rituals and had a deep reverence for their ancestors. Excavations have revealed the cremated remains of individuals and various grave goods, including pottery, beads and other artifacts.

Newgrange is not only a testament to the architectural and engineering skills of the ancient people who constructed it but also provides valuable insights into their beliefs, rituals and understanding of the cosmos. It is still an awe-inspiring site that continues to captivate visitors from around the world.

**Photos taken at The Boyne Valley, Newgrange, Co Meath.**

## Seasonal changes

Living on the farm, like any place in the Emerald Isle, we were at the mercy of the wild Atlantic Ocean. Autumn marked the return to school for a new year, a time that brought sadness and excitement all at once. Looking forward to seeing school friends after the long holidays, there was always lots of talking and catching up on holiday stories. The beauty of autumn colours as the trees shed their leaves in a bundle of spectacular colours intertwined – yellows, reds, orange, golden and brown. The air becoming crisp carrying the scent of the fallen leaves and the crunching sound underfoot. The ever-changing seasons played a big part in our life. Autumn changing into winter, creating a stark bleak picture with its bare trees, grey skies, chilly rain, sleet and snow.

My dad would be out working on the farm, tending to the animals who had now been moved from the fields to the indoor barns, to protect them from the harsh elements of winter. Dad would always be rugged up with thermals, several layers of clothing and at least two pairs of socks in his welly boots.

Spring and summer were our most favourite time of the year. School holidays were from June until September, and this free time was bliss, as we raced around the farm and fields around our home.

## Early years

I was a sensitive, intuitive and high-spirited child with a sharp memory of events as far back as when I was three years old. Our local school, Edengora School, was within walking distance from our home. I was very eager to get off to school with my three older sisters, and there were days when I escaped after my sisters, running down the road towards the school. My dad would take off after me on his bicycle and place me on the crossbar to ride back home again.

When I was just four years old and beginning my school journey, there were just two other girls in my class, Joan and Theresa. We would often spend our playtime hopping on the steps of the school and gathering under a majestic oak tree right in front of the building. However, one fateful day, during our break time, we made our way to the outdoor toilets. As I waited for my friends to finish up, I began jumping from the steps that led to the toilets, attempting to see how far I could push myself, and how long I could make my jumps. As the bell rang, signalling the end of the break, my friends hurried back to class. In a final attempt to show off my jumping skills, I took one last leap, only to tragically land in an open sewerage drain located in the corner. The drain was filled with dirty water, and I found myself completely submerged, my head included, in this foul-smelling mess. Miraculously, I managed to pull myself out of the drain. In a state of shock, I sprinted back to class without catching anyone's attention. I sat there for the remainder of the day, soaked in the contaminated water, and covered in filth, while the teacher remained oblivious to my condition. When I finally returned home from school, my mother was utterly taken aback when she saw the state I was in. She immediately undressed and washed me several times before allowing me to soak in a bath. As for the clothes I had been wearing, I'm not entirely sure what my mother did with them. She was understandably upset with the teacher for allowing me to stay in such a state until the end of the day, rather than having one of my older sisters escort me home. I know my mother had a meeting with the teacher to express her grievances, although I'm unaware of the specific details or the outcome of that conversation.

Not long after this incident the little country school was closed, and the pupils from the townlands in the area were taken to a bigger school closer to the local town. A school bus was arranged to drive around the countryside collecting us all. I remember feeling nervous about this new school. The first day we arrived in our new classrooms, I found two of my first cousins, Anthony, and Imelda, were in the same classroom. My cousin Imelda came to the top of the classroom, took my hand, and led me back to her desk to sit next to her. Imelda and I were friends right throughout our childhood and teenage years and we still hold a special bond, although we live on opposite sides of the world. Imelda and I would sometimes get into trouble for talking and laughing in class. We would often break into fits of laughter at the smallest thing and would not be able to stop laughing. We were separated from sitting next to each other several times. After a couple of days, we would approach our teacher and say, 'Please Miss may we sit together, we promise not to talk and laugh.' We would be reunited again until the next time we were separated. These are funny and very fond memories of my early years at school.

## Christmas time on the farm

Christmas time was always magical in the colder weather. At times we would have snow, creating a spectacular vision that would lift the spirits of even the faint-hearted. Christmas lights were a big deal in Ireland; the nightfall occurred so early in the evening, providing a beautiful sparkle of joy to our world as we prepared for Christmas time to celebrate the birth of Jesus. I loved Christmas time in our home. Mum would be baking Christmas puddings and cakes, fruit pies and there was always a great homely cooking and baking scent throughout the home. The kitchen aga stove was working overtime, as was Mum. Her baking was delicious, and there was always plenty to go around for family and friends who would visit over the festive season.

We eagerly received our gifts with excitement and gratitude. One of my most cherished Christmas presents was a doll nestled in a charming baby carriage. I delighted in pushing the pram throughout the house, tending to my doll by feeding and cuddling her. Another beloved gift was a complete tea set that brought hours of imaginative play. Engrossed in my make-believe world, I would brew imaginary tea and host delightful tea parties for my loved ones. These cherished gifts were treasured and cared for with great affection.

**The magic of garden snow.**

## Receiving First Holy Communion

I received First Communion at seven years old. After receiving the gift of First Communion we were taken to the local country pub, where we were treated with glasses of lemonade or orange to drink, lollies galore and gifted coins from everyone we met. Upon returning home, one of the first things we would do is count our coins. It was like a mini financial adventure, as we carefully sorted and tallied up the amounts we had received. This tradition of counting our earnings after the First Communion celebration became a source of excitement, curiosity, and even a bit of competition among siblings or friends who may have also received their sacraments and were curious about their financial gains.

This time was also significant as it often marked the beginning of opening a post office savings account. Our parents would guide us in understanding the importance of saving for the future, instilling in us the values of financial responsibility and preparing for unforeseen circumstances. It was a practical way to teach us about the concept of saving for a rainy day, laying the foundation for financial literacy and responsibility.

This combination of celebration, treats and financial lessons made the experience of receiving First Communion even more memorable and meaningful. It was a day filled with joy, generosity and valuable life lessons that would stay with us long after the excitement of counting coins and indulging in lollies had faded.

# Chapter 3

# What Happened When I Turned Eight Years Old

The intuitive ability of an eight-year-old came to light when I became ill, and the doctor sent me to hospital to have my appendix removed. On the way to the hospital, I remember saying to my parents, 'It is good that I have just appendix and nothing more serious and I will just have them removed, like Dad did a few years ago, and come home and everything will be fine.' As I said this, I had a strange deep knowing that it was not just appendix but something more serious.

I did indeed have my appendix out. My mum told me several years later, that I had woken up on the operating table during the operation, and they had to give me another anaesthetic. I had slept for days after the operation causing my parents a lot of concern.

# Down the Rabbit Hole and Back Again

I was happy and relieved to leave the hospital ward after this experience. I had a wound on my side that I knew about, it was painful, but I never complained. I remember it was June in Ireland and harvesting time was in full swing.

My illness continued after my return from hospital, it seemed like having my appendix out did not fix me. I was vomiting a lot unable to keep food down and I felt ill every day. The doctor sent me back to the hospital. The local hospital was in the town of Navan in County Meath about one hour from the farm. It was in some way soothing to know that my Aunty Kay, Dad's sister, was a nurse in this hospital, and she would pop in to see me regularly. Of course, my family came to visit me daily as well, mostly Mum and one of my sisters, as the others were back helping in the busy harvesting time on the farm.

I spent a month in hospital and was not getting any better. I was still vomiting and unable to keep food down. What was concerning was that the doctors were not investigating why I was ill. I just lay there in the hospital for weeks, begging my mum to take me home. Some of the sisters in charge were unkind and would say to me that 'I was not sick and should not be there.'

## Transfer to the Children's Hospital in Dublin

Eventually a specialist was called from the Children's Hospital in Dublin to examine me. One of the first things he did was to take my blood pressure and he was astonished at how high it was. He arranged for me to be transferred to the Children's Hospital in Dublin. I was hoping that I would be sent home, not taken to a hospital in the city, almost three hours away.

## What Happened When I Turned Eight Years Old

That evening my mum and my sister came to visit and were told I was going to be taken to the Children's Hospital in Dublin that evening. My Aunty Kay was there which was soothing for all of us.

A driver took us to the big hospital, and I remember being taken by wheelchair into an examination room. By this time, it was late evening, perhaps even night-time. The doctor told my mum, sister, and Aunty Kay to stand behind a curtain out of sight. He then proceeded to put his finger up into my back passage. I remember how much it hurt and felt uncomfortable. I felt scared. I have no idea to this day why he did such an examination. I did not experience this at any other time on an admission to hospital. We were then escorted to the ward where I would spend the next three months. I was placed in a room by myself with glass all around. A nurse came to settle me. My family had to leave as the driver was waiting to take them back to Navan. It was late now, as I could see it was dark outside. I felt fearful, panicky as I watched my family leave. I cried out for my mum and the kind nurse sat with me and soothed me and I instantly fell asleep.

I have some vivid memories of the time I spent in hospital as an eight-year-old. In the next room to me there was a small child in a cot. This child was physically deformed with a big head and small body. She did not make any sounds and just lay there in her cot all day and night. There was an energy around this girl that seemed to flow through the glass between our rooms. It was like she was communicating to me in some way, perhaps through her angels. No-one ever came to visit this little one.

I remember the rounds of blood tests, blood pressure readings and being wheeled off in a wheelchair for various tests. Some of these tests were distressing. I remember the first time I was taken to the procedure room and had a catheter inserted into my urethra; I was petrified. These procedures were carried out by what seemed like cold-hearted staff, and I was told to 'stop it' if I cried out in fear. There was no explaining what they were doing to me. I was like an object, a plastic doll lying there non-responsive. I learned very quickly to disassociate myself from whatever was happening to me to cope. When I was returned to my bed, I would pull the blankets over my head, sighing with relief that the procedure was over. My bed became my haven.

I was diagnosed with kidney disease that had affected both my kidneys. This caused my high blood pressure. My kidneys were very damaged and inflamed, and it took several months with lots of medication to resolve this, and to stabilise my blood pressure. I was prescribed steroids as this was the treatment to resolve inflammation in damaged kidneys. My body totally changed from the steroids, I was bloated all over, and I really disliked looking at myself in a mirror. For a couple of months, I was confined to bed and was not allowed to get up and walk around. This meant that I was not able to play with the other children in the ward. I was in a room by myself, and it felt isolating. As time passed one or two of the little girls in the ward would come into my room to visit me and they would bring dolls and toys to share.

My parents came to visit me every second day. It was not an easy task for them to travel up to Dublin, a five-hour round trip for them. I longed for their visits so much and the joy in my heart when they arrived. Leaving was not great, I hid my sadness well, as I knew Mum and Dad were also sad having to leave without me.

During the evenings when my parents couldn't visit, I was fortunate to have my two older cousins, Anne and Margaret, who worked in Dublin, come to see me. They were the daughters of my Aunt Rose, who was a beloved figure in our family. Anne and Margaret took turns visiting me during those evenings, bringing much-needed companionship and cheer. Unfortunately, my siblings were not allowed to visit due to a policy that restricted children visitors. However, my cousins had a creative idea to bypass this rule.

Anne and Margaret had a younger sister named Trasa, who happened to be the same age as my oldest sister, Rosemary. Determined to see me, they concocted a plan to dress up in adult clothes and makeup, to pass as grown-ups. One memorable Sunday afternoon, they entered my hospital room, along with Mum and Aunt Rose, dressed in elaborate outfits, adorned with makeup, and even wearing high heels.

It was quite a comedic sight to behold, as these young girls transformed themselves into mini adults for the purpose of visiting me. Their dedication and enthusiasm brought a much-needed sense of joy and laughter to that hospital room. We shared a wonderful afternoon, filled with jokes, laughter, and the bond of family. Their visit remains a fond memory of that time, reminding me of the love and support that surrounded me, even during challenging circumstances.

On the weekends I would have more family visitors, all my aunts, uncles and older cousins came to visit on a Saturday or Sunday. I received bundles of get-well cards from everyone in my family and community. These cards were stuck up on the glass between my room and the little deformed girl's room next door. There were so many cards that they completely blocked any view either way. I remember my sensitivity around this and feeling sorry for this little girl. At least she was able to see into my room when she was turned on her left side, and at times her wide eyes would appear to look in my direction. It was as if we were able to communicate through the energy fields between us.

# Down the Rabbit Hole and Back Again

On a few occasions my siblings came to the hospital, and I was taken to see them in a wheelchair, to an area close to the entrance. I remember seeing my sisters and brother sitting along in a row and feeling so foreign to them. It felt like I was a different person than the little girl who entered this place. The happy little girl who was once a big part of our family life on the farm, now feeling emotions with no name. Deep emotions of aloneness, abandonment and just longing to see the countryside, and our home on the farm again.

## The hospital school

As the months of July and August passed, September arrived, signalling the return to school. I yearned to be reunited with my dear friends, especially Imelda, and to see her happy smiling face once again. The hospital ran their own in-house school. Since I was confined to bed, a teacher would visit my room to go through lessons with me and assign homework. However, it felt as though all the knowledge I had previously acquired had slipped from my mind, and the tasks ahead seemed daunting and challenging. It was the first time in my young life that I developed a dislike for school.

However, there was a glimmer of hope when the doctor granted me permission to start getting up and moving around. The first time I stood up, I felt a rush of dizziness, nearly toppling over, but with time and adjustment, it became easier. As I regained mobility, I was moved from my own bedroom to a shared room with another girl. This change brought me great joy, as I had the opportunity to make friends with other children in the ward. Now that I was no longer confined to my bed, I was also able to attend the school within the hospital. Unfortunately, I have no pleasant memories of the teachers who taught us. The stress and pressure of the school environment led me to withdraw and become non-verbal as a coping mechanism.

# Chapter 4

# Making Sense of it All

The impact on the whole family when a child is diagnosed with a chronic illness is a topic that has been extensively researched. Numerous studies, such as 'Chronic Illness in Children' from the Association for the Wellbeing of Children in Healthcare, have shed light on the challenges and effects that such illnesses can have on both the child and their family.

Reflecting on my own experience, I realise that while I was focused on my own struggles during my hospitalisation, it wasn't until later that I recognised the impact it had on my parents, sisters and brother. The frequent hospital visits meant that my parents were often taken away from home, causing a sense of loss and disruption to their daily lives. I now wondered how they managed to support a sense of normality while dealing with my illness and running the farm and the household.

## Down the Rabbit Hole and Back Again

The research into the impact of childhood illness and hospitalisation on families confirms that these experiences are not surprising. Siblings, like my sisters and brother, also faced challenges during this time. They may experience a loss of time spent with parents due to the long drives and hospital visits. Questions arise, such as who would help on the farm or with cooking meals, highlighting the added burdens placed on the family.

## Sibling memories

*'It was summertime, and I was nine years old when Breda went to hospital. It was a warm summer evening when I went with our mum to visit Breda. We stopped to buy 99 ice-creams cones to take one to Breda. On arrival we found that Breda was terribly ill and had to be transferred to the Children's Hospital in Dublin. The sudden change of plans caused significant emotional distress for everyone involved. Our Aunt Kay, who happened to be on duty, came to offer help and support. We arrived in Dublin and after some time of waiting in corridors, we were taken back to Navan in a taxi, where we then got our car and drove home. It was now 2am and as we got closer to our home, we saw our dad pacing up and down on the road, not knowing what had happened. The absence of communication tools like telephones meant the rest of our family were unaware and worried. It was a time of sadness and overwhelming stress for our family.'*

*'This was the start of a three-month separation from our little sister. All the extended family and neighbours rallied around us; helping with travel to visit Breda, so Mum and Dad did not have to do all the driving. On the weekend we*

*would all pile into the car for the trip and us kids would wait in the car outside the hospital while our parents went inside to visit. After some time, there was great excitement as we were told that Breda would be able to come out to the reception area to see us. We were eagerly waiting when Breda arrived in a wheelchair. Breda looked different as she was very bloated from all the medications and was a sickly pale colour. We were all incredibly quiet not knowing what to say. It was a brief encounter and a sad one after all the anticipation.'*

*'We missed our little sister. It was summer and we had our school holidays, and we would normally have been running freely in the fields. As young children we did not understand what was wrong with Breda, and why it was taking so long for her to be well and home again.'*

*'The house was chaotic as Mum and Dad were constantly busy trying to get the farmwork done early to get on the road to the hospital. Our aunts and uncles called in to see us a lot. As religion was important there were a lot of masses and prayers to attend. It was a period of constant worry. Even our dog sat outside our bedroom window every night and cried endlessly. This stopped the very day Breda returned home!'*

*'During that summer in 1970 it felt like there was an empty space, a hole we felt as Breda was missing from our summer day adventures. It felt like a long time without Breda. When Mum and Dad would visit Breda during the week, we would be taken to our Aunt Rose's house, and she was always so kind to us kids.'*

# Down the Rabbit Hole and Back Again

*'One vivid memory I have of the time Breda spent in the Children's Hospital is one Sunday, when Mum and Dad were visiting, and us kids were waiting in the car. When our parents emerged from the hospital, they were both in tears, overwhelmed with emotions. I also recall the evenings after all the jobs on the farm were done, Mum and Dad would head off to Dublin to visit Breda, in the family car which was an Austin A40. I would worry about their safe return.'*

*'Eventually there was great excitement and preparation for Breda coming home. Breda had a special armchair, and Dad made a little table to go across the front of it. Breda would sit in this chair and do her painting, drawing, colouring in. It seemed like it was her happy place. We all treated Breda very preciously until she got into her normal life, around our home and school. I remember how protective I felt of Breda, and especially when she returned to school.'*

These memories and experiences highlight the profound and lasting impact that chronic illness can have on a child and their family. It underscores the strength and resilience of families who navigate through such challenging times, relying on the support of loved ones and the community around them.

Listening to my siblings' recollections of this time indeed brings about feelings of sadness. It is natural to reflect on the impact of illness on the family and to have a sense of gratitude for the conversations that have taken place. Opening up and discussing these experiences, even if they might be difficult or painful, is a crucial step towards healing. It allows for acknowledgement and validation of the emotions and experiences that my siblings and parents went through at this time.

## Making Sense of it All

While the research conducted didn't provide any surprises regarding the impact of childhood illness on the whole family, it's important to note that everyone's experience is unique. Hospitalisation experiences for children in 1970 would have been vastly different from what they are today. Acknowledging the impact of my illness on my family and recognising the support systems that contributed to my resilience have been important steps in my healing journey. Sharing my story and experiences helps to create understanding and empathy and may provide solace to others who have faced similar challenges.

# Separation anxiety

I remember I struggled with separation anxiety every time my parents left after a visit. I was frightened of some of the medical staff, and I was traumatised by some of medical procedures and invasive treatment experiences. I certainly displayed many of the behaviours of a traumatised child; detached, distant or out of touch with reality. In the early weeks after my discharge from hospital, my separation anxiety manifested in intense emotional reactions when my parents left home. I would yell, scream and cry if Mum and Dad left home to go anywhere. I remember I would stand on the front doorstep screaming and crying, the pain I experienced on these occasions was intense. These behaviours eventually faded away as I settled back into family life and returned to school. Despite the limitations imposed by my illness, I had a strong desire to fit in and to be part of the family, part of the class, rather than being singled out.

My resilience was solid, and had grown from living in a supportive, warm, and loving family. Within my family I felt loved safe and secure. In addition, our family's connection to the community, having aunts, uncles and lots of cousins around me gave me a keen sense of belonging.

# Chapter 5

# Growing My Armour and Resilience

In this chapter, I will delve into how my experiences during my illness and recovery helped me develop a stronger sense of resilience and a metaphorical armour to face future challenges.

As humans, we often underestimate our capabilities until we are faced with difficult circumstances that leave us no choice but to rise above them. This is especially true when it comes to children who confront their fears alone. It is important to recognise that it can be cruel to ask a child to stop crying when they are going through challenging experiences. For instance, during my time in the Children's Hospital, I underwent various medical procedures such as IV insertions, blood tests, IVP X-rays, and other invasive tests – it should be completely acceptable to cry and feel scared. Crying can be good as it can help a child release the strong emotions of fear and panic. Reminding kids in hospital that they can be brave and scared at the same time, they are not alone, and there are hands to hold are extremely important. These comforting words and gestures are so important when caring for sick children.

When I was finally discharged from the hospital in October 1970, I noticed a stark change in my personality. The traumatic experiences I had endured had transformed me from the carefree and happy-go-lucky girl I once was. I had developed coping mechanisms such as disassociating and relying on non-verbal communication. Consequently, I returned home as an extremely timid and introverted child, burdened by the multitude of medication I had to take. My mother used to jokingly say that I would 'rattle' due to the sound of all the pills.

Upon entering our home back on the farm, I couldn't help but feel that the house had somehow shrunk compared to my memories. The wide and extensive corridors in the hospital had become my new norm, and it took time to readjust to the familiar surroundings of home. Initially everything felt strange. I needed time to adapt to the familiar routines, mealtimes, and medication schedules. My mum, understandably protective after the ordeal we had been through, kept me home from school for a few weeks. Eventually, she allowed me to return to school but insisted on picking me up at lunchtime.

As time went by, I gained more confidence and asked to stay at school for the entire day. I slowly settled into the school routine, taking the bus with my sisters and brother, and enjoying more time with my friends during recess. Of course, regular checkups at the outpatient department of the hospital and visits to our local GP for ongoing care were part of my life.

## Growing My Armour and Resilience

By sharing my journey of overcoming fear and adversity, I hope to shed light on the importance of acknowledging and supporting the emotional needs of sick children. It is vital to provide them with reassurance, understanding that bravery and fear can coexist, and offering a helping hand to hold during their challenging times.

# Hole in my Soul

*There is a hole in my soul, and that's okay*

*This wound is the place where light enters.*

*A healing bright light*

*Illuminating, shining bright*

*With love and peace.*

*Refreshing me all through my body*

*My heart and my soul.*

*Regenerating the woundedness buried so deep.*

*Wrapping and embracing the beauty*

*My inner child drenched in sad tears*

*Fragile and pure*

*Within a grown-up body and that's okay*

*Protective and honest to my core.*

## Second admission to the Children's Hospital

When I was approximately ten years old, I was hospitalised due to a necessary change in my medication. This adjustment required close supervision, as I was being weaned off steroids. Fortunately, the side effects of bloating that I had experienced gradually dissipated, filling me with a sense of my old self. During this time, I spent around a month in hospital, but it was not all gloom; in fact, it was getting closer to the festive Christmas season, and the ward was bustling with preparations.

The spirit of the holiday season infused the atmosphere as we adorned the ward with colourful decorations. I distinctly remember the excitement building up as we eagerly awaited the arrival of Santa Claus. Despite the constraints of hospital life, I felt a newfound sense of freedom during this hospitalisation. One of the benefits was the opportunity to venture outside to the playground area, where I could run, play and enjoy the company of the other children. It was during one of these playful afternoons that an unexpected incident occurred.

As I played on the play equipment, a boy from the same ward approached me and unexpectedly planted a kiss on my cheek. This surprise gesture left me momentarily shocked and unsure how to react. Without thinking, I instinctively jumped up and scurried back inside the ward. Little did I know that this innocent act would have unforeseen consequences.

Unbeknownst to me, the head nun of the ward had seen the playground activities from the window. Witnessing the unexpected kiss, she took it upon herself to punish me for this innocent act. As a result, I was relegated to the boiling hot laundry room each afternoon, tasked with ironing bed linen for one to two hours. I cannot recall if

45

my retribution was imposed on the boy involved. However, it seemed that I bore the brunt of the blame for this incident.

Despite this disheartening turn of events, the anticipation of being discharged on Christmas Eve overshadowed any lingering resentment. The prospect of returning home and reuniting with my family filled me with excitement and joy. But before my parents arrived to collect me, a magical surprise awaited us in the ward.

Santa Claus himself paid a visit to the hospital, igniting an atmosphere of immense excitement and delight among the children. However, the sister nun who had previously punished me acted once again by casting me aside from the festivities. She declared that I was too old to partake in the merriment and sent me back to my room. It was disheartening to see other children my age happily taking part while I was left excluded, as if being punished once again for a simple innocent gesture.

Nevertheless, the warmth and love that enveloped my family home during the Christmas celebrations allowed me to swiftly put these experiences behind me. As I now reflect upon my encounters with the sister nuns, a blend of emotions emerges. While many of the sisters showed compassion and kindness, there were others who exuded a cold and heartless exterior. Although time has likely separated these sister nuns from our world, I extend forgiveness and healing to their spirits.

Later in life, during my university studies, I delved into the realm of human psychology. This exploration supplied valuable insights into the intricacies of unresolved past experiences and their everlasting impact on our inner selves. It highlighted the profound effect such experiences can have on our interactions with the world around us.

In conclusion, my journey through the hospitalisation during my childhood, though fraught with moments of both happiness and persecution, has shaped me in ways that propel me toward understanding and empathy. It has allowed me to recognise the complexities of human behaviour and the significance of healing and forgiveness in our personal growth.

## Final admission at the Children's Hospital

At the age of eleven, I found myself once again admitted to the hospital, this time for cardiac tests. Living with high blood pressure, which was managed through medication, my heart would often pound in my chest with a rapid rhythm. The relentless burden placed on the heart by high blood pressure can lead to heart disease and even heart failure if left unaddressed or if pressure fluctuations occur. To prevent any potential complications, the medical team decided on an angiogram – a procedure that would provide crucial insights into my condition.

Having an angiogram at the tender age of eleven was yet another invasive and traumatic experience. Back then, these procedures were performed through the groin, an intricate process that required a delicate touch and careful explanation. Unfortunately, no-one took the time to fully explain the procedure to me or provide reassurance about what I was about to undergo. I was simply prepared for the procedure with a gown and hat and then whisked away to the procedure room, leaving me feeling anxious and bewildered.

As the needle punctured my left groin area, a sharp sting of pain shot through my body. I could feel a tube being inserted, slowly snaking its way up inside me. Fear consumed me as I lay on the hard table, enduring what seemed like an eternity. There was no attempt by the medical staff to communicate with me or offer any words of comfort amidst their casual conversations with each other. I felt like a lifeless doll, undergoing what could very well have been an experiment. The isolation and lack of empathy intensified when I was strapped down to the bed and left alone while the staff took their lunch break. It was a demoralising experience, one that stripped away my sense of humanity and left me feeling utterly unimportant.

When the staff finally returned and the results of the procedure were checked, the tube was removed from my body, and the incision in my groin was carefully stitched up. I retreated to the sanctuary of my hospital bed, burying my head under the covers, exhausted and weary from the ordeal. Fortunately, the results came back positive, and I didn't require any further heart procedures. As sleep overcame me, I sought solace in the knowledge that this hospital admission was coming to an end.

During the discussion with my doctor and parents at the conclusion of this admission, the topic of my upcoming twelfth birthday arose. As the Children's Hospital catered specifically to younger patients, it was decided that I would be referred to an adult hospital for my future care. This marked yet another significant change for both my family and me, a transition that we needed to navigate and adapt to. An appointment was scheduled for me to attend outpatients at Jervis Street Hospital in Dublin. Although the hospital's location presented challenges with parking, its proximity to the bustling city centre meant that most visits to the outpatients were followed by a bit of shopping – a small silver lining in the midst of adjustments.

The move from the children's hospital to the adult hospital marked the end of an era for me and my family. It required us to confront and embrace new surroundings, medical professionals, and approaches to care.

## Transitioning to an adult hospital

My first inpatient admission into the big adult hospital was when I was twelve years old. I had become ill with a nasty kidney infection that was so severe I needed intravenous antibiotics. I remember that feeling of overwhelm when I was admitted to this strange place. I was placed in a small children's ward where there were children from babies to toddlers and all ages up to twelve. The closeness of the ward created a noisy and interactive environment. Each room had at least two beds if not three. I loved to play and carry the little ones around and found myself just loving those tiny little ones. I would take a baby or toddler into my arms to soothe and hug them if they were sad or hurt.

There was this twelve-year-old boy, let's call him Jack, who ended up becoming my buddy during our time in the hospital. We would chat for hours, finding ways to pass the seemingly never-ending time. And let me tell you, with my extensive family tree and a whopping sixty first cousins, hospital stays were never dull. My cousin Rose, who happened to be the older sister of my school friend Imelda, would make regular visits after finishing her shift at Cleary's Department Store nearby.

One fateful afternoon, Jack called me into his room. Oblivious to any strange intentions, I sat down at the end of his bed, naively thinking we were just going to have another one of our long chats. But boy, was I wrong. Out of nowhere, Jack unexpectedly pulled me down on top of him and started yelling for help, pretending he was being attacked. The poor nursing staff rushed in, finding me trying to untangle myself from the situation. I quickly explained what had actually transpired and that Jack had pulled me down on top of him. Feeling a mix of emotions, I retreated back to my room, deciding to stay put for the rest of the day.

Later that evening, Rose came to visit me, providing some comfort, in the midst of the chaos. Little did I know that another surprise was awaiting me. The nursing staff approached me while Rose was still there, saying I needed to gather my belongings as I was being transferred out of the children's ward and into the adult ward. I was dumbfounded, questioning why I was being moved and not Jack, who had caused all the commotion. It was a humbling and humiliating experience, as if I had done something wrong, even though I was completely innocent. On top of that, I was overcome with sadness at the thought of leaving behind the little ones I had grown accustomed to playing with.

Accompanied by Rose, I made my way to the female adult ward. It was a vast space with several beds, filled by elderly ladies. As I glanced around, my emotions bubbled up and my face turned a bright shade of red, probably because I couldn't take in any fresh air. The trauma of the whole ordeal pushed me into a state of dissociation, causing my body to freeze up. After a reluctant goodbye from Rose that evening, the nurse came to take my blood pressure. It was alarmingly high, raising concerns among the medical staff. The doctor swiftly decided that I should be transferred back to the children's ward immediately, recognising the distress I was facing.

In summary, it was a roller-coaster of events that brought about confusion, resentment, and ultimately, a realization of the need for proper care and understanding in such sensitive situations.

# Chapter 6

# Those Teenage Years

During my high school years in the convent, I found myself adapting well to the bustling atmosphere of the school. It was the year 1974, and although Imelda and I were placed in different classes, we remained great friends. In my own class, I made new friends with Patricia and Loretta. Imelda made new friends also and we all gathered in the schoolyard during break times. On cold and wet days, we would find refuge in one of the classrooms.

I enjoyed high school and despite facing challenges such as frequent illnesses and hospitalisations, I managed to do well academically. Kidney infections were a regular occurrence for me, resulting in missed school days and the need for antibiotics and bed rest for about a week. During these sick days at home, I felt isolated from my friends. Upon returning to school, I would have to catch up with the lessons and activities I had missed. However, my resilience helped me navigate through these difficulties.

It was during the long summer school holidays that I had a memorable encounter. I met a girl named Anne while she was on vacation at her cousin's house, which was situated on a hill overlooking the bridge that crossed the river stream. This bridge served as a meeting place for young people from the local area. On warm summer evenings, we would congregate at the bridge, socialise, and engage in activities such as skipping stones, searching for tadpoles, and daringly trying to cross the river by stepping on the rocks.

Anne and I became great friends during that time, and she lived in Co Laois, which is in the midlands and south of Dublin. Whenever school holidays arrived, I would manage to hitch a ride with my sister's boyfriend, who worked in sales and travelled across Ireland. Anne and her twin brother Eamonn and I would spend our time together listening to music, visiting local pubs, and attending concerts throughout the summer.

One of my fondest memories with Anne was when we hitchhiked around the enchanting Ring of Kerry and camped out. The scenery along the Ring of Kerry was simply breathtaking. Whenever we pitched our tent, we would often meet other campers and strike up conversations. Many young people from Europe were travelling around the country during those years. Our adventures often led us to local pubs with live music, where we enjoyed the company of both locals and fellow campers. Throughout these years, I felt like a typical teenager, except for the fact that I always carried a bag of medications to manage my health. These medications helped with my urinary functions and blood pressure control.

# Those Teenage Years

Anne and I were friends for many years. Sadly, Anne passed away in a drowning accident at the age of forty-four. Hearing the news of her untimely death deeply affected me. It was difficult to fathom that she was no longer with us. Anne had always been kind, jolly and a wonderful friend to me. May she rest in peace.

**My dear friend Anne and me (RIP dear friend).**

After experiencing various teenage crushes, I met a local boy named Patrick who became my first real boyfriend. Patrick came from a farming family in a nearby townland. He owned a motorbike and would often visit me after school and on weekends, taking me for rides on his bike. Our relationship lasted for several years, spanning from 4th to 5th year. The final year of school, 5th year, was when we prepared for our Leaving Certificate exams.

# Down the Rabbit Hole and Back Again

Towards the end of our time in school, I would stay home from the Sunday night dances to focus on my health and studies. Unfortunately, during one of those dances, while I was absent, Patrick met another girl and started a relationship with her without my knowledge. For a period, he was dating both of us simultaneously, unbeknownst to me. When the truth eventually came to light, Patrick ended our relationship, leaving me utterly devastated and heartbroken. I had trusted him completely and the betrayal reopened the wounds of my childhood trauma, evoking feelings of abandonment. My sensitive soul felt irreparably wounded.

During this challenging period, I turned to writing as a form of healing. Putting my emotions and thoughts on paper helped me navigate through the pain and begin the process of healing my wounded heart.

## Teenage First Love

*Bring me just a single daffodil from the meadow*

*Does it still glisten with the morning dew?*

*And in the evening, when the sun is setting,*

*Does the meadow's soft untouched grass*

*Miss the soft thread of us*

*Barefoot runnin?*

*And then feelings sinking*

*The soft summer breeze cooling us.*

*I long to be in love again like it was*

*Among the grass and trees*

*And simple things.*

*To sleep so calm in the moonlight*

*So happy.*

*And with the dawn*

*Another carefree day.*

*I loved you well,*

*Will the threads ever come together?*

*Do you ever remember?*

## Dream Catcher

*Maybe if both our dreams were entwined*

*We would both reach the end in our search*

*For the good things in life?*

*I want to run wild through the trees*

*The half-forgotten leaves of autumn,*

*Will they remind me*

*Of my half-forgotten past?*

*Now thoughts, who am I?*

*Dreams, what would I like to be?*

*Of people, of friends*

*Where to go?*

*What to do?*

*Where might*

*This road lead me too?*

# Chapter 7

# The Troubles in
# Northern Ireland

It was not my intention when beginning to draft my story, to touch on the times of the Troubles in Northern Ireland. However, the Troubles were very much alive in the 1970s and although our family were not directly affected, as we lived in the Republic, the news brought the sad reality of this war into our home.

I have tried to supply a lay person's narrative that has somehow helped me to try to understand all the questions such as the whys, whats and wheres. This is also to show respect to all those directly affected by these times, including innocent children.

## A brief history of The Troubles

The English invaded Ireland in the 12th century and maintained control in Ireland for 800 years. They were interested in controlling Ireland for reasons including economic, political, and religious; to take over ownership of the land in Ireland that was seen as a valuable resource. At the time Ireland was mostly Catholic and the English tried to anglicise the Irish population and suppress Irish culture.

Between 1845 and 1852 Ireland suffered a period of starvation, disease, and emigration, which became known as the Great Famine. Remember that at this time Ireland was part of the United Kingdom, which was the richest and most powerful nation in the world. Ireland was producing a surplus of food and massive quantities were being exported to Britain. Between 1845 and 1852, more than 1.5 million Irish people starved to death. Another 1.5 million had no choice but to emigrate to foreign lands. The famine left a scar so deep within the Irish people, which set in motion a war that would finally gain Ireland its independence from Britain in 1922.

The Great Famine of Ireland is memorialised in many locations throughout Ireland, especially in those regions that suffered the greatest losses. Shrines are also displayed in cities overseas, with large populations descended from Irish immigrants. To date more than 100 memorials to the Irish Famine have been constructed worldwide.

# The Troubles in Northern Ireland

## Famine Cauldron from soup kitchen Memorial in Dunshaughlin, Co Meath.

The Anglo-Irish Treaty of Independence 1922 marked the end of the Irish War of Independence and the beginning of the Irish Free State.

The Treaty also set the stage for the division between Ireland and Northern Ireland. The unionists in Northern Ireland (who were predominantly Protestant) wished to maintain the union with Great Britain.

This division led to a troubled history, including violence and political tensions between the late 1960s and late 1990s.

During this war, some 3,600 people were killed and more than 30,000 were wounded.

The saddest stories have been told of these times. At least 186 children, aged 16 and under, lost their lives because of the Troubles. We can never really know what it was like for those families living in the war, the gunfire, the army just barging into homes and shooting, bombs up the street. Children survived the deaths of mothers and fathers, brothers and sisters, best friends. These were very tragic and sad times for Ireland and particularly for Northern Ireland.

## The influence of music and musicians

Music was an outlet for many during The Troubles. Many artists from the Irish Republic and Britain took it upon themselves to raise awareness of the issues and plead for peace. Rock and roll became an outlet for bands to express their sentiments about the world in which they lived. Family favourite artists include The Cranberries, The Police, U2, Paul McCartney, and his band of the times, Wings.

In February 1972, Paul McCartney released a single called 'Give Ireland Back to the Irish' with his band Wings. This song was written by Paul McCartney and his wife Linda in response to the events of Bloody Sunday, on 30 January that year. British troops in Northern Ireland shot dead thirteen civil rights protestors. The song was banned by the BBC for its anti-Unionist political stance, but still managed to reach No. 16 in the UK, and No. 1 in Ireland.

# The Troubles in Northern Ireland

It was a tough time especially for those who lived in Northern Ireland. It is also worth noting that in County Meath, we were friends with families who were Protestants, and we were Catholics. One of the local farming families who were Protestants were in our home regularly and were our buddies within the farming community, and we helped each other out in any way we could.

# Peace

The Prime Minister of the United Kingdom, Tony Blair, played a significant role in the Northern Ireland peace process during his time in office. His involvement and leadership were instrumental in bringing about the Good Friday Agreement of 1998, which marked a historic milestone in the efforts to achieve peace in Northern Ireland. Blair set up close working relationships with key political figures in Northern Ireland, including Sinn Fein leader Gerry Adams and Unionist leader David Trimble.

Blair's approach to the peace process was characterised by active diplomacy and a willingness to engage with all parties involved including the Irish government.

One of the most significant achievements of Blair's tenure was the Good Friday Agreement, which was reached on April 10, 1998. The agreement set up a power-sharing government in Northern Ireland, with provisions for cross-community cooperation and the recognition of the region's dual British-Irish identity. It also addressed key issues such as policing, justice, and human rights.

The Good Friday Agreement stood for a crucial step towards ending the violence and political deadlock that had plagued Northern Ireland for decades. While the peace process faced challenges and setbacks in the years that followed, the agreement laid the foundation for a more peaceful and stable Northern Ireland.

## President of Ireland Mary Robinson (1990–1997): Reflections on working towards peace

Mary Robinson was the first female to hold office as President of Ireland (1990–1997) and was one of Ireland's most popular presidents. As President of Ireland and United Nations High Commission for Human Rights, Mary Robinson has done so much for Ireland.

She engaged in the decriminalisation of homosexuality, the legalisation of contraception, the legalisation of divorce, enabling women to sit on juries and securing the right to legal aid in civil legal cases in Ireland. In 2004, Robinson received Amnesty International's Ambassador of Conscience Award for her work in promoting human rights.

Her reflections include:

*'So many divisions and at so many levels, between rich and poor, between women and men, between different religions and ethnic groups, between citizens and migrants. These divides are at the core of so many of today's conflicts. A common thread in each situation was an unwillingness on both sides to see "the other" or "the enemy" as an individual with hopes and dreams, and with equal rights. If the problems are so clear, why does it continue to be so difficult to act differently, to be inclusive of our human family?'*

# The Troubles in Northern Ireland

The Dalai Lama emphasises with his message:

*'The practice of compassion, love, and kindness. Compassion can be put into practice if one recognises the fact that every human being is a member of humanity and the human family regardless of differences in religion, culture, colour, and creed. Deep down there is no difference.'*

In essence, humanity shares one world. The world does not need divisions that lead to conflicts. Brotherhood and sisterhood, sharing compassion and kindness towards each other, an inclusive human family; a peaceful world for everyone.

I fondly remember phone calls with my mum who would always talk about President Mary and what she was doing for women and progressing the rights of women in Ireland. I was quietly so proud of my mum as she was giving insights into her inner world and her own beliefs around equality for women in society.

In one of my melancholy days following a news headline around The Troubles, describing more bombings and killings, I took myself off to my favourite meadow and wrote about my special place.

## My Peaceful Meadow

*Falling into the deep, a meadow enclosed by trees, coloured by daffodils,*

*Green and gold.*

*Could our country be confined to just one meadow*

*So beautiful, so peaceful.*

*No sounds but the birds, the flowing stream nearby.*

*All peoples together, no bombs, no gunfire.*

*I dream of joining all good people together in the meadow of peace and love.*

*Let power depart, greed and selfishness lost forever.*

*And let sharing be the only word spoken, all guns must be broken,*

*Man will have no need to fight.*

*Peaceful soft breezes, flowing freely in the meadow of our lives.*

*Peace please always stay.*

*I love you so.*

## The Troubles in Northern Ireland

## Insights into our First Nations

While the Australian story is unique, it also shares similarities with our Irish history. To complete the chapter, I will explore the rich heritage of the Aboriginal and Torres Strait Islander people, sharing an overview of the learnings I have gathered since my arrival in Australia in 1987.

Prior to arriving on Australian land, I had never heard about the Aboriginal people, the First Nations people of this country. Any time I viewed photos of Australia, they depicted the beautiful beaches, and the unique wildlife, mainly kangaroos and koalas.

I have learned the history of Aboriginal people throughout my time living here. I took an Aboriginal Studies module during my studies at university. Since this time, I have collaborated with Aboriginal people in several roles, both as colleagues and as clients. There is so much that we can learn from the Aboriginal culture, spiritual beliefs, and connections to their lands. I would like to acknowledge and honour the Aboriginal and Torres Strait Islander people, by supplying some background information from my own perspective.

Aboriginal and Torres Strait Islander peoples are the first peoples of Australia, meaning they were here for thousands of years prior to colonisation. There are varying estimates for how long Aboriginal and Torres Strait Islander peoples have lived on this continent, however, upwards of 60,000 years is what current research reveals.

Aboriginal and Torres Strait Islander peoples have diverse and distinct cultures, languages, beliefs, and practices. They lived in harmony with the land and had a rich and complex ritual life.

# Down the Rabbit Hole and Back Again

In 1770, Lieutenant James Cook claimed the east coast of Australia for Britain, despite the presence of Aboriginal peoples. He declared the land as terra nullius ('no-one's land'), which ignored the Aboriginal sovereignty and ownership of the land.

In 1788, the first fleet of British convicts, soldiers and settlers arrived in Sydney Cove, marking the beginning of the colonisation of Australia. The arrival of the Europeans brought diseases, violence, dispossession and oppression to the Aboriginal peoples, who suffered a drastic decline in population and loss of culture.

The colonisation of Australia was based on the doctrine of discovery, which gave Britain the right to acquire and govern the land. The British government did not recognise the Aboriginal peoples as the original owners of the land, nor did they make any treaties or agreements with them.

The colonisation of Australia had a devastating impact on the Aboriginal peoples, who were subjected to massacres, removal from their lands, forced assimilation, discrimination and marginalisation. Many Aboriginal children were taken away from their families and placed in institutions or with white families – they are known as the Stolen Generations.

The Aboriginal peoples resisted the colonisation of their lands and fought for their rights and recognition. Some of the notable events in the Aboriginal history include the Frontier Wars (1788–1934), the Day of Mourning (1938), the Freedom Rides (1965), the 1967 Referendum (1967), the Tent Embassy (1972), the Mabo Case (1992) and the National Apology (2008).

Today, Aboriginal and Torres Strait Islander peoples make up about 3.3% of the Australian population. They continue to celebrate their cultures, languages, and identities, and to advocate for their rights and interests. They also face many challenges and issues, such as health, education, employment, justice, reconciliation and self-determination.

In my experience working with our First Nations people, both as colleagues and as clients, I embrace and value their way of being in this world. Building effective partnerships with Aboriginal colleagues is an ongoing process that requires genuine effort, humility and respect.

# Chapter 8

# Renal Failure and Dialysis

After successfully completing my Leaving Certificate, I was thrilled to secure a position in the accounts department at a local factory. However, my excitement soon turned into a struggle as I found myself dealing with various health issues.

My health was declining, making it incredibly difficult to get through the workdays. I would feel extreme fatigue and nausea. When I would return home, all I could manage was collapsing into bed and sleeping. Unfortunately, my health took a further downturn, and I fell ill not just once, but twice during my brief time at the factory. Both instances resulted in severe kidney infections, requiring me to take time off work to recover.

# Down the Rabbit Hole and Back Again

Just prior to completing three months at the factory, I received an unexpected summons to the office. My manager and a senior manager expressed their satisfaction with my work performance but raised concerns about the frequency of my absences. They asked if I could guarantee them that I would not need as much time off in the future. Stunned by the question, the only response I could muster was, 'Nobody can guarantee that they won't get sick.'

As a result, they insisted that I visit their company doctor for a medical evaluation. Unfortunately, based on the doctor's report, the decision was made to terminate my employment on the grounds of my health condition. To be honest, there was a sense of relief within me, as I was extremely unwell at that stage, burdened by continuous bouts of nausea and fatigue.

During the months of September and October 1980, I was in and out of the hospital in Jervis Street. I was told by my doctor that I was likely to enter end stage renal failure and I needed to be prepared for dialysis treatment. My sister Trish was studying nursing, and she was working at Jervis Street, and it was nice to have her close by.

In September, they put a fistula in my left arm, as this was the process of preparation for dialysis where they connect a vein to an artery. When this connection is created, fast flowing blood from the artery travels up the vein. The vein adapts to this by gradually thickening up and enlarging and turns into a 'super-vein.' At this point, the fistula is strong enough to withstand needling on a regular basis and allows for regular dialysis. However, the fistula did not work on my left wrist, and I needed another procedure to create a fistula in my right wrist. Thankfully, this one worked. The fistula site is important to have an easy way to get blood from your body, through the dialyser, and back into your body.

# Renal Failure and Dialysis

When the fistula is working effectively, you will find a strange buzzing sound. If you place the wrist close to your ear it will sound very loud like waves on a beach. It was quite fascinating and as time progressed the veins in my arm and hand became quite large.

In October, I was transferred to yet another hospital, St Mary's in the Phoenix Park, Dublin. I remember the evening I was sent there, my sister Rosemary was visiting me, and we were packed off together in a taxi. I could tell that Rosemary was in shock and everything felt strange that evening. My body felt bloated from fluid buildup, at times it felt like I was hallucinating but I also had a strange peaceful feeling.

The next morning, I was started on dialysis. The fistula in my wrist had not developed enough to take the needles and the nurses tried several times to get my veins to cooperate. It was so painful, and my arm was just black and blue after this. I had to have a temporary shunt placed in my upper chest, so I could start dialysis. After the shunt was inserted, I bled so much that I needed a blood transfusion.

After a few weeks of using this temporary shunt I got infection in the site, and I had a roaring temperature. This meant it needed to be removed and they once again started to use my arm fistula, which I was very tentative about. Eventually my veins grew to ease this process, but I stayed in hospital until December to monitor the dialysis.

As usual in my fear or moments of sadness I would take pen to paper and just write.

## My Hospital Bed

*Tonight, I am living within*

*The dark shadows of life,*

*Will the sunshine through – maybe tomorrow*

*And if not*

*Will there be another 'morrow.*

*Then I may understand*

*Yet even deeper than before,*

*The beauty of life.*

*As the glaring sunlight is once more*

*Softened*

*By the patterns of shadows.*

*Do I really need to talk*

*For this ink and paper*

*Can entangle my mind.*

*Will it send me to sleep untroubled?*

*I feel a deep fear*

*Like a child afraid of darkness.*

*My weary head lay down*

*I need to rest awhile.*

# Renal Failure and Dialysis

When I was discharged from hospital it was arranged that I would stay in Dublin with my sisters to alleviate the travel to and from the hospital. Attendance for dialysis was required on three days a week for four to five hours and took place at the hospital in a dialysis centre. Dialysis requires considerable time and effort. In addition to the considerable time spent travelling to and from appointments and receiving treatment itself, people receiving dialysis must carefully monitor their diet and fluid intake. It is a lot of work, and it takes time to adapt to the changes.

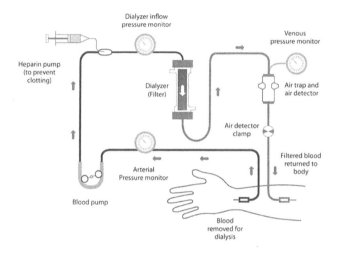

**Diagram of a Hamodialysis machine.**

Side effects of dialysis included:

- Blockage in your vascular access site (entrance point)
- Muscle cramps
- Hypotension (low blood pressure)
- Weakness, dizziness, or nausea
- Blood loss

# Down the Rabbit Hole and Back Again

The muscle cramps in my feet were excruciating and unfortunately, a common occurrence among people undergoing dialysis. It was not uncommon to hear someone scream in agony from the pain of these cramps. Luckily, the nurses were well-versed in providing assistance during these episodes. They would allow some fluid into your body and apply pressure to your foot to alleviate the cramp. Although it was a temporary relief, it supplied a much-needed respite from the intense discomfort.

After dialysis sessions, I felt weak and drained. In those days, it felt like dialysis stripped away the goodness from your body, and the lack of vital nutrients caused post dialysis fatigue. Despite this, I would make my way to the bus stop, where I would catch a bus back to my sister's place. The journey made for challenging walks, but I persevered.

Diet played a crucial role in managing my condition. I had to adhere to strict restrictions on what I could eat. My daily fluid allowance was limited to just 1 litre, which included all liquids I consumed. Foods high in potassium were off-limits, as were sauces, as they increased fluid intake. Dairy products were also prohibited. My sister Rosemary, being the amazing support system she was, cooked meals that adhered to my dietary restrictions with great care.

I have since learned that advancements in dialysis treatments have included the reinfusion of nutrients into the body before the end of the procedure, which provides a significant boost. It is heartening to know that medical advancements have made the dialysis experience more manageable and less depleting.

During those nine months, I relied on dialysis to keep me alive. There were undoubtedly tough moments, and my life at nineteen was far from ordinary compared to that of my friends. Writing became an

# Renal Failure and Dialysis

outlet for me to express my thoughts and feelings. I found solace in putting pen to paper and documenting my experiences. It was during one afternoon, after a dialysis session, that I was mistaken for a drug user by a shopkeeper due to my bandaged arm and visible veins. I took the opportunity to explain my situation to him, and he genuinely listened and apologised for his assumption. It was a small encounter that reminded me of the importance of spreading awareness and educating others about dialysis and its impact on individuals like myself.

By sharing my story and writing about my experiences, I hope to supply a glimpse into the challenges and triumphs of life on dialysis.

# Down the Rabbit Hole and Back Again

## Just a Sunday afternoon

*I sit here in this park – it's a Sunday afternoon,*

*The sun shines bright, and everything seems perfect.*

*I listen to the sound of children playing,*

*The gushing of the stream*

*And swaying of the trees.*

*I watch the lovers pass by*

*And this entire world just seems so perfect.*

*But I know it's not perfect.*

*For me, I live on a kidney machine.*

*My diet is restricted, no ice-cream or soft drinks,*

*Arms torn and bruised from shunts and large needles.*

*No not a junkie!*

*For tomorrow I must go and sit on a dialysis machine*

*To watch my blood cleared from the poisons that have accumulated.*

*And when it's over feeling so weak and weary*

*Walking to the bus stop arms bandaged tight.*

*Through the city crowds*

*And tomorrow a free day to be grateful for*

*Before my return.*

## Renal Failure and Dialysis

## The power of intuition and spirituality in my life

This time in my life was a painful time. I experienced pain and struggles most days. I took life one day at a time and I relied on my family to prop me up by their love and support. Pain is difficult to understand or put into words; it seems to be one of those mysteries with no rational explanation. Spiritually I felt good and mentally prepared for death should it come. Many of my fellow kidney patient friends passed away. A little girl passed on the train with her mum on the way to dialysis. Life was fragile over this time, and I treasured each day.

Intuitively, I knew somehow deep inside that for me, this stage was the beginning of the end of this part of my life and that I would get through this well. These feelings came even prior to conversations about having a kidney transplant.

When I could manage to get home to the farm on a weekend, I would go to my favourite places in nature. The riverbank or the meadow where I could find solace. Being one with nature brought a profound sense of peace, an awareness of the interconnectedness of all living things. This experience was therapeutic. It was on one of these occasions a voice came to me telling me everything was going to be okay. It is incredible how our intuition can guide us, supplying a sense of hope and resilience during challenging times.

Once again, I used pen and paper to write about my experience. I experienced great comfort through my writing, allowing me to express my deepest thoughts and emotions, refilling my resilience bucket.

## A Prayer in Nature

*As I sit here in the sweet meadow*

*Darkness almost upon me.*

*For all my senses I am thankful!*

*For I can hear, I can feel, I can smell, I can touch.*

*I can sense the beauty of nature around me.*

*Can there be anything more beautiful*

*Than the song of the birds at dusk!*

*The homecoming with their little ones,*

*Food and love and warm nest hugs!*

*It is here in this beauty of nature*

*I feel the presence of the Higher one.*

*The purest love.*

*I hear the gentle whisper in my ear*

*Telling me*

*'Things will be alright, have faith in me.'*

*For the beauty of nature surrounding me*

*The fields of green,*

*The hills and mountains,*

*The seas and rocks.*

*Your highest glory shines onto us,*

*Let not man destroy such beauty!*

# Chapter 9

# Kidney Transplantation

The transplant team rallied our family together to discuss perhaps an option to have a sibling donate a kidney to me. All my family went through the tests to check compatibility, and astonishingly, my sister Philomena was a perfect match. And so it was.

Things seemed to move rapidly. My sister had more tests to ensure that all was well for her to undergo the surgery. It was June and the operation was set for June 16th. Mixed emotions flooded my mind. I was elated yet extremely anxious, especially for my sister and how she would cope with such a major surgery. During that era, kidney donation involved a full-blown incision across the side and back, unlike the minimally invasive keyhole surgery available today. Given the depth of the surgery, recovery could be a painful and lengthy process.

## Philomena's memory of this time

*'When we all were tested to see if we were compatible for donation, I seemed to intuitively just know that I would be Breda's donor. It was not for me a hard decision as I could see how hard dialysis was on Breda and she had lost so much weight. Of course, being young and fearless helped. I was filled with trepidation when it came time to be admitted to hospital. I was completely healthy, so it was a weird experience going into hospital. The hospital experience and care I received was incredibly positive. Then seeing how well Breda responded made it all worthwhile. I was sore but it was summer, so we enjoyed the lovely weather recovering at home on the farm.'*

## Sibling memories of the day of the transplant

*'We gathered home on the farm on the day of the transplant. We were all very distracted and we kept busy cleaning the home and washing all the bedlinen and clothing around the home. It was like a spring cleaning to erase all the negative energy from our home and to provide a fresh and healthy new start'.*

*'In the early evening, our kitchen was full of relatives and neighbours, providing support and all eagerly waiting for news from the transplant surgeries. At around 7pm our mum made one of many calls to the hospital on that day. On returning to the kitchen, she burst into tears and said the kidney is functioning. There was an emotional outburst of joy from everyone in our kitchen that evening and not a dry eye in the house'.*

# Kidney Transplantation

Unfortunately, my sister experienced significant pain after the operation. Going into hospital without any previous illness and waking up from such an intense surgery was undoubtedly a traumatic experience for her. Philomena had several months off work to recover following this ordeal.

After the successful transplant, I experienced a whirlwind of emotions. We were told by the medical team that my sister's kidney started working immediately. I felt an overwhelming sense of relief and gratitude. Having a fully functioning kidney to filter toxins and excess water from my body made me feel incredibly good. With this joy, a significant wave of guilt washed over me, knowing the pain, and suffering my sister endured to provide me with this gift. Unavoidably, I found myself questioning my decision to accept her kidney, resulting in an ongoing internal struggle.

Throughout our recovery period, my sister and I found solace in the serene environment of our farm home. The tranquil surroundings provided a sense of comfort and peace, particularly enhanced by the delightful summer weather. As we gradually regained our strength, a remarkable transformation occurred within me – the guilt that had burdened me for accepting my sister's kidney began to dissipate, replaced by a profound sense of joy and gratitude for the newfound lease on life I had been granted.

My kidney twin sister Philomena (left) and Breda (right).his photo was published along with an article about our transplant in a local newspaper.

# Kidney Transplantation

## The Gift of Life

*The greatest gift I did receive*

*From my dear sister*

*Philomena.*

*I like to walk through the meadows*

*To the riverbank*

*Where I sit and reflect.*

*The birds they come say hello*

*And how is your day.*

*I feel so free*

*No longer living on a machine.*

*Eat the ice cream, drink soft drinks!*

*So much choice beyond my dreams.*

*For I received the greatest gift*

*A gift of life, a perfect match kidney.*

*To say thank you is never enough*

*Because the pain you went through*

*To give me life again; and I want to tell the world*

*Just how good I feel.*

## Down the Rabbit Hole and Back Again

*Philo you are my happy go lucky*

*Loving sister.*

*Even with the pain you did not forget your smile.*

*I wish and pray for you*

*For all the good things that you love.*

*May life's road be always pleasant*

*And kind to you.*

*Thank you and I love you*

*My dear twin kidney sister.*

# Chapter 10

# New Beginnings – Finding My Feet

After receiving my sister's precious gift, a kidney, I experienced a newfound sense of vitality and wellbeing. For the first time in what seemed like forever, I felt truly alive. The burden of kidney disease and the accumulation of toxins in my body had left me feeling constantly unwell. But now, it was like a miraculous transformation. I no longer needed to undergo gruelling dialysis treatments or endure the discomfort of large needles piercing my veins. The blood tests I had to undergo post-transplant seemed insignificant compared to the procedures I had endured during dialysis. My arms, once wounded and weary, finally had a chance to rest and recover.

# Down the Rabbit Hole and Back Again

The freedom I felt was indescribable. I had so much more time on my hands since I no longer had to spend long days at the dialysis centre. I could eat and drink whatever I pleased, without restrictions. It was liberating. As time went on, the dosage of my anti-rejection medication was significantly reduced, a testament to the perfect match that my sister's kidney was. With the newfound lease on life, I began to gain a healthy weight. Prior to the transplant, I had weighed only around 45kg. Moreover, as my leg gradually recovered from the nerve damage that occurred during the surgery, I started walking and gradually increased my exercise capacity.

The local community took a keen interest in my story, supplying an opportune platform to raise awareness about the incredible benefits of organ donation. My sister and I were interviewed for the local newspaper, and our story, along with a photo, was published. It was heartening to see the impact that our journey had in spreading awareness and encouraging others to consider becoming organ donors.

While on the path to physical recovery, I also faced the challenge of finding stable employment in Ireland during the 1980s. Securing positions in government and banks was a laborious process with numerous stages and multiple interviews conducted by executives. It was an incredibly daunting and stressful experience. At that time, it was often said that success in finding employment relied more on who you knew rather than solely on merit. Fortunately, our family had a relative who was a bank manager, and he was contacted on my behalf. With their support, my family was confident that I would be offered a job in a bank.

I vividly remember the day of the interview, feeling nervous and overwhelmed. As I entered the interview room, three executives sat on chairs at one end, while a single chair was placed about two feet away from them. I felt small and insignificant as I walked towards the chair, guided by one of the men's gestures. In a moment of awkwardness, my handbag plummeted to the floor. It was one of those mortifying moments when all I wanted to do was run out of the room and the building. I scarcely recall the rest of the interview, the questions I was asked, or my own responses. Unfortunately, I was not offered the position at the bank, and everyone around me was devastated on my behalf.

I coped with this disappointment by turning to my writing. In my heart, I knew that my tribe, the group of people who would understand and accept me, was out there somewhere. I embarked on a quest to find them, documenting my journey in a piece I titled 'Searching for My Tribe.' It was a profound realisation that my true tribe was waiting to be discovered, and I was determined to find them.

## Searching for My Tribe

*My mind running on*
*Like the river's flowing waters,*
*Sometimes deep, sometimes shallow,*
*Sometimes stormy, sometimes calm,*
*Sometimes wild and clear,*
*Sometimes dull and dark.*
*It seems never-ending.*
*And yet just thoughts*
*Running on, on, on ...*
*Until alas ... reaching the ocean;*
*The crashing sea waves,*
*Whirling against the rivers flow.*
*A weakness!*
*Rebelling in vain*
*And so they unite.*
*The hesitancy of the river*
*Resembling my own,*
*Resembling my weaknesses;*
*An unexpected downfall.*
*And so upon the ocean*
*We sail together in my dreams.*
*And yet endless doubts*
*A fear divides me.*
*Can we be overruled by power?*
*Presently I resign*
*And silently watch and despise.*
*Yet a knowing that*
*'The future brings brighter things to mind.'*

It was widely known in the transplant community that individuals who had received kidney transplants were facing challenges in securing employment. While it could not be dismissed as mere speculation, it seemed possible that discrimination was at play. Regardless, one thing was certain – this situation caused considerable stress and affected my sense of self-worth, leaving me feeling somehow flawed, even though my health was on par with that of any other person.

After several months unemployed, I eventually had an interview with The Medical Board of Ireland and was offered a position as a receptionist. This job not only provided me with the necessary means to build a new life but also offered me the independence and resilience needed to thrive in the face of adversity. Finally, I could lead a life that approximated 'normal' – whatever normal may be? I worked, socialised with friends, attended parties, exercised, indulged in my favourite TV shows, and returned home to the comforting love of my family on the farm most weekends, rejuvenating my spirit.

## Meeting my future husband

At the age of twenty, I met my future husband, Cathal, who was kind-hearted and caring. It happened during a motorbike rally one summer evening in June. I was with my sister and her partner. On the journey to the event, I took the opportunity to drive their car some of the way. When we arrived at the village I had to brake suddenly because there were guys playing soccer on the road. As I braked, I noticed one of the guys had captivating bright green eyes that held my gaze briefly. After a day filled with action and activities, we all gathered around a campfire as the night grew colder. Cathal ended up sitting next to me, and I mentioned that my feet felt chilly in my open-toed sandals. Without hesitation, Cathal went to his tent and returned with a fresh pair of socks for me. This small act of thoughtfulness filled me with joy and marked the beginning of our blossoming relationship.

## Other family events

Rosemary and her family emigrated to Australia whilst Philomena and Trish spent some years travelling and working overseas, before returning to settle in Ireland with their families.

Meanwhile back in Edengora, Philip and his family have continued the farming traditions of our family, now six generations on this land. The farm has evolved and grown throughout time, yet still has the familiar landscapes, colours, textures and smells that flow through each season in the beautiful Emerald Isle.

# Chapter 11

# Participating in the World Transplant Olympics

In the early years following the transplant, I was involved with the Irish Kidney Association around events and fundraising. The topic of the World Transplant Olympics (now known as the World Transplant Games) was discussed. It was 1984 and the games were to take place in Amsterdam in September that year. Past participants were looking for new members to join their team and I was approached as a possible candidate. As I had been taking safe care of my health, eating well and exercising, I agreed to join. Over that summer the eight members in our team would meet regularly to train. We were provided with a coach. One of the members worked close to me and he would collect me from my office at lunchtime and drive us to the racing track nearby, where we would practise our runs. I was entering into athletics track and field and swimming. We were provided with dress suits for the opening ceremony and march, as well as sportswear for the events.

I felt so proud as I marched into the stadium with our team members, Irish flag leading. It was an amazing feeling and one that has stayed with me for my life. There were twenty-two countries represented at these games and the atmosphere was electric.

So, the games began. I competed in track and field, mini marathon 5km and came second. I took part in 1500m, and I came second. Finally, the last day we entered the 4 x 400m mixed relay with two guys and two girls, finishing first. This was just the icing on the cake. We were all so proud.

I will never forget the closing ceremony where they held a massive banquet for all involved in the games. We were called to stand on the podiums like the real Olympics to be presented with our medals. I received two silver and one gold medal, and I was bursting with pride in my achievement.

This photo was taken outside the Medical Council, my workplace in Dublin. I was presented with flowers and a beautiful Waterford Crystal bowl from my work colleagues. I still have it on display in my home.

# Participating in the World Transplant Olympics

Proudly showing off my medals.

In addition, our community at home in the country congratulated me for my achievements in an event where I was presented with a lovely piece of jewellery.

Following the Olympic games, I continued to train and the following year I completed a half marathon in Dublin and raised money for the Kidney Foundation. It was my mum who did most of the fundraising around our local community and I just loved how my mum was on board with me. It was a great bonding experience for us both.

## Down the Rabbit Hole and Back Again

## Reflections on the World Transplant Games: A journey of resilience and hope

In April 2023, Australia hosted the World Transplant Games, an event that captured my attention and interest. I closely followed both the Irish and Australian teams, who performed remarkably well throughout the games. Their outstanding achievements left a lasting impression on me. The World Transplant Games in Perth were undeniably a resounding success, and Transplant Australia released an article recently to highlight the importance of the Games:

*'In the aftermath of the World Transplant Games held in Perth, Australia in 2023, the event continues to spread positive messages about the lifesaving impact of organ transplantation. More than six months have passed since the Games, but their influence persists. As Australia prepares for Thank You Day, a significant occasion, a special and inspirational documentary titled "Second Chance Champions" will be broadcast on free-to-air television on November 17th and 19th. Produced by Dentsu Creative, the documentary chronicles the journeys of three organ recipients and one living donor who participated in the World Transplant Games. The focus of this documentary is to shed light on the lives of those who have directly benefited from organ and tissue donation. By sharing their stories, these individuals aim to inspire more Australians to embrace the importance and beauty of organ donation. Furthermore, early next year (2024), the documentary will be made available internationally on Paramount Plus, ensuring that its powerful message reaches a global audience. This documentary serves as a remarkable tribute to the profound impact of the World Transplant Games and showcases the*

## Participating in the World Transplant Olympics

*inspiring stories of those who strive to participate in the spirit of the gift of life. It demonstrates the transformative power of organ donation and the profound gratitude felt by those who have been given a second chance.'*

# Chapter 12

# Getting Married and Immigrating to Australia

In 1985 Cathal and I became engaged and in 1986 we were married. This was a beautiful day that I will always treasure.

# Down the Rabbit Hole and Back Again

**Our wedding day with my family.**

Cathal and I had discussions about visiting my sister and her family in Australia, which sparked our plans and excitement for what this trip might entail. However, there were numerous factors to consider, with my health being the most significant one. With my regular check-ups at the renal unit, where they monitored my blood results to ensure everything was functioning properly, I had grown accustomed to a certain routine. Fortunately, my kidney function remained perfect, which gave us the confidence to go ahead with our plans.

We decided to apply for a twelve-month working holiday visa for Australia because it presented us with the perfect opportunity to not only spend time with our family but also embark on an exciting adventure and see if we would enjoy living there. Our visa application was approved, and in February 1987, we experienced both happy and sad moments as we said goodbye to our loved ones and left behind

## Getting Married and Immigrating to Australia

the freezing temperatures and snow-covered landscapes. Upon our arrival in Adelaide, Australia, we were welcomed by our family and the sweltering heat that reached 34 degrees Celsius. This extreme change in weather was just the beginning of our Australian journey.

**Cathal and I off to Australia 1987.**

Australia quickly became our home, and we embraced the warm weather and the opportunity to shape our lives as we saw fit. The freedom to create our own path was exhilarating, and Australia certainly lived up to our expectations with countless opportunities waiting to be seized. I secured a position at a psychiatric hospital working in administration. Cathal, being an electrician, found employment swiftly. We moved out of my sister's place and settled into a rental property not far from her home, marking the beginning of our new lives in Australia.

## Down the Rabbit Hole and Back Again

While we missed our family back in Ireland, communication was limited to expensive landline phone calls, and we relied heavily on writing letters to stay connected. Despite this, we adapted to our new lives in Australia. In our first year, my parents had the opportunity to visit us, which was an incredible experience for all of us.

**One of my favourite photos of Mum and Dad in Australia.**

## Australian permanent residency and citizenship

As our working holiday visa approached its expiration, we applied for permanent residency, with Cathal's employer sponsoring us. The biggest hurdle in the process was my health, as I had to undergo a medical examination. I had developed a good rapport with my renal specialist, at the Royal Adelaide Hospital. He supported our application providing a sound medical report. We were successful in achieving our permanent residency and some years later we went on to obtain Australian citizenship, becoming what is known in Australia as 'Skippies.'

## Settling into Australian life

With our residency secured, we took the next step and purchased our first home, complete with its own swimming pool. It was a delight to come home from work on summer evenings and take a refreshing swim. Swimming was a passion of mine. Towards the end of 1989, we travelled back to Ireland for my brother's wedding, bringing along our nephew, Paul, for an unforgettable experience. Celebrating Christmas, New Year and the wedding allowed us to enjoy a festive time filled with joyous celebrations and gatherings.

In December 1990, we were blessed with the arrival of our first child, Jordan Patrick. Given my medical history, I never thought I would safely experience pregnancy and childbirth, so this was a moment of immense gratitude and happiness. Our second bundle of joy, Dion Charles, came into our lives in September 1993, completing our family of four. Our home was now filled with a sense of wholeness and love.

**Our boys Jordan and Dion.**

# Chapter 13

# Dad's Passing

When you live on the other side of the world, it is always a terrible shock to receive a phone call informing you that a loved one is ill. In April 2006, we received such a call. Dad had suffered a stroke and was gravely unwell. Without hesitation, we swiftly made our plans to fly back home, just in time to be there, in Edengora, when Dad passed away. He was eighty-eight years old.

The experience of being present at Dad's passing was nothing short of extraordinary. It is difficult for me to put into words, but I will try my best to describe it. I remember standing at the top end of his bed, with my hand gently resting on his, whispering soothing messages into his ear. As he took his final breath, I witnessed something truly remarkable. I saw his spirit rise up from his body, a radiant white light ascending towards the heavens. I could sense the presence of someone waiting to greet Dad, and I strongly felt that it was his mother. In that moment, an overwhelming feeling of joy, love and peace enveloped me. It was unlike anything I had ever experienced before. It felt as if I had caught a glimpse into the afterlife. All I could do was gaze up at Dad's radiant spirit, seeing his happiness and serenity, and simply smile. Love and gratitude flooded my heart for having been granted this extraordinary experience. Initially, I assumed that everyone in the room must have shared in this divine encounter, but it soon became clear that this was not the case. I felt immensely grateful to Dad for bestowing upon me the gift of this profound experience, as it truly felt like it was gifted to me by him.

After returning to Australia following the funeral, Dad visited me once again, this time in the form of a spirit. I woke up one night to find his luminous presence shining down on me. It was an awe-inspiring, dazzling light, and the overwhelming feeling that washed over me was one of pure love and tranquillity. I wished for that feeling to stay with me forever, for it was so joyful and ethereal. Once again, it felt like Dad was giving me a precious glimpse into the next life. It felt like his way of reaching out to me and reassuring me that he was at peace.

In the years preceding Dad's passing, as his health declined due to arthritis and his mobility became increasingly limited, I wrote a poem expressing the sadness I felt witnessing his aging body.

## Dad's Passing

## To my Dad

When I know that we will never see again
some happy bygone days

I feel sad inside.

For today I see you grow old and weary from
the laden work on hand.

Do you feel life passing quickly by

Or do you feel so weary that you'd like to rest awhile.

And yet what must be done tomorrow

Is what you're thinking of,

And I wonder why you strive.

I love you so and I wonder do you know?

We often speak in our own way it's a special gift we share,

Your calm unselfish ways I will remember 'till my dying day.

Even though you are a man, I see you as a child inside

And when one day you meet the Lord

He will take you as his child,

And all weariness will be washed away.

And then one day

I hope and pray we will all be together again,

In our new world of peace and joy.

# Down the Rabbit Hole and Back Again

The poem allowed me to capture and process the emotions that came with seeing Dad's physical struggles. It served as a tribute to his resilient spirit, even in the face of adversity.

Dad's passing was a deeply profound and transformative experience for me. It not only taught me to cherish the moments we have with loved ones but also opened my eyes to the possibility of a spiritual existence beyond this life. Dad's spirit continues to live on within me, reminding me of the boundless love and peace that await us all in the afterlife.

# Chapter 14

# Return to Study

During this period, my life seemed to be guided by something greater than myself. Returning to study and being accepted into the Bachelor of Social Work program at the University of South Australia felt like being carried on the wings of an angel. It's hard to put into words, but I had an intuitive sense that I was being led down this path by a higher power. Everything seemed to flow effortlessly, and I excelled in my studies, achieving my bachelor's degree in 2008.

After completing my bachelor's degree, I continued to deepen my knowledge and skills by pursuing postgraduate studies in counselling. Later, I also obtained a qualification as a mindfulness meditation teacher. I was eager to gain experience in a range of areas that would allow me to help people, so my new career took me on a diverse journey. One of the organisations I worked with was Catherine House, a shelter for homeless women. There, I saw the remarkable resilience of the human spirit as I supported women who had faced immense challenges in their lives, including domestic violence, addiction, child removal by Child Protection and homelessness. It was incredibly rewarding to witness their strength and see how they could transform their lives and find their own paths to flourishing and reaching their potential.

From there, I worked in a community mental health program, parenting programs, and in addiction counselling and rehabilitation. My own experiences as a child, which showed me what not to do when working with families, strongly influenced my approach. Inclusive practice became an essential aspect of my work with families facing challenges in various aspects of their lives. It is crucial for practitioners to engage not only with caregivers but also with children themselves. Children need protection, kindness, and compassion to see the world as a safe place. For younger children or those who struggle with verbal communication, play therapy, such as sand play therapy, can be a powerful tool. It allows children to express their psychological overall wellbeing through non-verbal means. This therapy helps children bring forth strong emotions, aiding their understanding of how they are feeling and coping. Validating and honouring their experiences is key, as staying silent about their struggles can be detrimental and hinder the healing process.

Throughout my career, I have seen the incredible strength and resilience of individuals, families and communities. It continues to inspire me. The role of a social worker is not only about support, but also about empowering individuals to find their own strengths and resources. It is a privilege to be able to walk alongside others on their journey towards wellbeing and fulfillment.

# Return to Study

During my time working in a parenting program our work was featured in media as part of Child Protection Week awareness during this time.
https://centacare.org.au

## Making moments

A parent's love shapes a baby's mind.

Supporting mothers to understand this connection and nurture secure attachments with their baby is Breda McAlinden's role. The children and families worker visits young parents who may be at risk of peri-natal depression or anxiety, and often are experiencing other mental health challenges.

**Me in my role working with children and families.**

# Down the Rabbit Hole and Back Again

Breda (pictured) works alongside new and expecting mums – and their families – to increase their self-belief, capacity to parent and understanding of what their baby needs, and when.

'Being able to recognise your baby's cues can be really empowering for a young mum, especially if she is low on confidence and is relatively unsupported,' Breda says.

'It stops that spiral downwards that can start if their baby is really unsettled and they're not getting any sleep. A lot of the mums have experienced trauma and sadness in their own childhood. If they don't have another template for parenting, it can be really difficult to know how to respond to and soothe their baby which is how trust develops in that first year of life.'

## Responsive, sensitive parenting gives a baby's brain the message that the world is a safe place

Breda highlights the program's focus on parenting education – delivered primarily through visual tools – and the small victories she sees families achieving with each home visit.

'We meet some amazing and strong women,' she says. 'They come a long way. Some will tell you they don't know how they would have got through tough times in life without our support, so that speaks for itself.'

# Chapter 15

# Grief and Loss

I believe that our childhood wounds can have an impact on our intimate relationships. I can honestly say this from my own experience, as I found myself reliving some of the traumas from my childhood illness in my marriage. I carried with me feelings of fear, abandonment, unworthiness, and a sense of invisibility, much like the rubber doll in the treatment rooms. I lacked validation and the list of negative experiences seemed endless. All these experiences brought tremendous turmoil to my sensitive soul, eventually leading to my first-ever experience of panic attacks.

During this challenging time, I found myself alternating between fighting and freezing. I started therapy with a psychologist and later asked my husband if he would be open to having couples' therapy. This never eventuated due to a lack of commitment through this process. The pain became unbearable, and I eventually made the difficult decision to separate from my husband after 25 years of marriage. I never believed it would be a permanent separation, as I hoped we would take a break, come together, and discuss our problems and find resolution. Unfortunately, this never happened. My husband entered a serious new relationship that progressed rapidly, and they began living together.

I used my writing to manage my big emotions over this sad time in writing about my sensitive soul.

# My Sensitive Soul

*Would you share with me some thoughts?*

*Of things which make you laugh*

*Of things which make you cry –*

*I cannot reach this mountain top*

*To look upon the shore,*

*For you have taken me halfway*

*And now I cannot go alone.*

*Come*

*Maybe we can reach the top*

*Have no fear!*

*For I am just a child at heart*

*On life's pebbly path.*

*If you help me reach the top*

*Maybe I will grow,*

*And with your strength*

*And no Fear I could go alone.*

# Down the Rabbit Hole and Back Again

After being separated from Cathal for about five years, we never officially divorced, the devastating news came that Cathal was diagnosed with cancer. During this time, I felt left out as he had a new lady taking care of him. My heart ached, and all I wanted was to be by his side, holding him and providing care. I couldn't help but blame myself as well. Although Cathal had been a smoker, he had quit years before our separation because I had constantly encouraged him to do so. However, I later discovered he had returned back into the harmful habit.

Furthermore, Cathal's diagnosis was bowel cancer, and I couldn't help but think that if we were still together, I would have ensured he underwent the testing that is sent out to all individuals over fifty years old. Cathal wasn't particularly mindful of his health and rarely fell ill. The journey through cancer was one filled with immense pain, gruelling treatments, weight loss and invasive surgeries. At this time, our oldest son Jordan was overseas. He had been travelling and was in Ireland, where he had spent two years working. Our younger son Dion had a girlfriend Karolina, and together they brought our little Iggy into the world. In a time of such sadness and pain, Iggy brought us all tremendous joy, as he continues to do to this day.

After the diagnosis, my dear husband suffered immensely, fighting the battle against cancer for over three years. His health deteriorated, and he looked ill, but he somehow managed to keep his jovial nature and find positivity in life's brighter side. We began to worry about Cathal's impending death, and calls were made to bring Jordan back to Australia. At that time, he was travelling and had detoured to India, where he ended up being grounded for five months due to Covid. Fortunately, Jordan made it home just six weeks before his father passed away. I was grateful that he made it, not only for his own sake but also to provide support for his younger brother

# Grief and Loss

Dion, who had endured the years of their father's illness and its impact without the bond of his brother to share and support each other through.

Cathal passed on 15th December 2020, at just fifty-nine years. It was a devastating blow to all our families both here in Australia and overseas.

Cathal and our boys, 2002.

The boys and Mum, 2014.

Dion & Iggy, 2021.

# Grief and Loss

**Nanna & Iggy – my pride and joy.**

My Grief Poem to honour my husband for 25 years and the father of our precious children was read by Jordan at his dad's memorial.

# Down the Rabbit Hole and Back Again

## Grief Poem

*Dearest Cathal,*

*We came together when we were young, just 20 and 21.*

*We grew up together until we parted at 50 and 51.*

*A lifespan of 30 years; so much to honour and respect.*

*Our early years in Ireland on motorbike and country roads*

*Venturing further with bike and tent travelling
through UK and France.*

*You loved me and I loved you.*

*Cody your furry four-legged friend was of course your first love.*

*We married in the fall of '86; with family, friends and not
forgetting your four-legged furry friend.*

*A wedding album still intact; glowing happy faces; full of pride.
We were so young and full of life; dreams for our future and
having little ones.*

*Across the globe we came from Ireland, leaving behind family
and the winter snow fields of '87, arriving to the intense heat of
an Australian summer.*

*Geoff and Rosie, Paul & Laura were our anchor; we landed, and
we stayed.*

*Together we built our new lives with
excellent opportunities all around.*

*We worked and worked and soon we bought our first house
and a year later we had our first bouncing baby boy, our darling
Jordan brought us so much happiness and joy.*

*These days were long and happy as we loved our baby boy.*

# Grief and Loss

Our second beautiful baby son Dion came into our lives; the grief of his early arrival and lung condition was soon replaced by his dynamo personality; a little guy with so much umph and giving us all so much joy.

And later our four-legged baby Cooper joined the family, a tiny puppy. On that Saturday afternoon you said you were going with the boys to the "man's shop" (Bunnings), returning some three hours later with puppy in a box.

There are so many fond memories of our family life together.

Travelling back across the globe to Ireland
to show off our boys.

Together we watched our boys grow, learn and play.

There were soccer games, and practice (you coaching), Saturday tennis, Sunday cricket and little athletics.

Our lives were busy, and content.

We loved to entertain, summer BBQs and Sunday roasts.

Having family and friends around

Red wine and jokes

You always the positive larrikin everyone loved.

You loved your music ... From Phil Coulter, John Denver, Neil Young (to name a few), Anja and the beautiful Celtic sounds playing gently in our home. The piano became your new toy as you played with no need for music notes or lessons, but from your heart your tune just flowed.

In the dusk of life, before we knew it, our boys had grown into young men.

And then surprise along comes our grandson our little Iggy McAlinden. Your name and legacy will live on forever in our little man with the biggest heart I have ever known. I am grateful that

# Down the Rabbit Hole and Back Again

*we have known the love of having a grandchild and Iggy will forever remember you.*

*And now I feel numb; regrets and never really knowing how we parted at 50 and 51.*

*I loved you when were 20 and 21; as I loved you when we were 50 and 51.*

*I have loved you all the years we have been apart, and my wish would have been to look after you when you became so ill; but this was not meant to be.*

*The pain of your illness it took its toll; so much suffering you endured.*

*Our boys so distraught!*

*Today we take solace, no more suffering Our Dear Beloved.*

*Just like a child enters this life; those who pass go as little children sent.*

*And for us who grieve may:*

*Warm summer sun, Shine kindly down,*

*Warm wind blows softly here*
*Good night, dear heart,*
*Good night, good night.*

# Grief and Loss

## So much grief and loss

I have experienced an immense amount of sorrow and heartache as I lost my husband and then my mother within a span of eighteen months.

The era of Covid brought about a great deal of separation among people, including work colleagues, families and friends. For those of us with elderly relatives, it was an especially stressful time. My mother had been diagnosed with dementia and eventually needed full-time care, leading to her admission into a local nursing home. I had a strong desire to visit her, but due to travel restrictions, flying was simply not an option.

During this time, I wrote a letter to my mum and sent it to her, along with some cherished photos from our shared memories. My sister informed me that Mum was absolutely delighted to receive this heartfelt letter. I was immensely grateful that I had sent this to her, not knowing at the time that she would be soon leaving this earth. In February 2022, we received the call that our mum had a serious fall and was in hospital. Fortunately, it was just at that time that Covid restrictions eased, and flights resumed. I made it home and spent ten precious days with Mum before she peacefully passed away. Once again, I find myself immensely grateful for the time we had together.

*Dear Mum,*

*I want to express how much I love and miss you. It's hard to believe we are living in a time when we can't fly home to see you. Not a day goes by without thinking of you, and I pray that you are safe and in good health. I can picture you sitting in your favourite chair by the kitchen table, always offering cups of tea and food to anyone who visited. The memories of sitting around that table with you, enjoying tea and scones, and the peacefulness and serenity of the beautiful countryside surrounding us, are treasured. I also appreciate how you cared for our dogs, they were your special companions and protectors. Oh, how I long to be there with you in the kitchen of our life. I miss you deeply.*

*Lots of love from your daughter,*

*Breda*

## Grief and Loss

## Mum's Celebration of Life Ceremony

Our mum was given a great send-off memorial service, and her grandchildren took a big part in this. Reading messages of hope, singing beautiful songs, and reading poetry. The poem that follows is a very beautiful, piece and so perfect for our mum. It was read at her memorial by her grandson, Jett.

## *A Mother's Crown*

*Heaven lit up with a mighty presence,*
*as the Angels all looked down.*
*Today the Lord was placing the jewels*
*Into my mother's crown.*
*He held up a golden crown,*
*as my darling mother looked on.*
*He said in His gentle voice,*
*'I will now explain each one.'*
*'The first gem,' He said, 'is a Ruby,*
*and it's for endurance alone,*
*for all the nights you waited up*
*for your children to come home.'*
*'For all the nights by their bedside,*
*you stayed till the fever went down.*
*For nursing every little wound,*
*I add this ruby to your crown.'*
*'An emerald, I'll place by the ruby,*
*for leading your child in the right way.*
*For teaching them the lessons,*
*That made them who they are today.'*
*'For always being right there,*
*through all life's important events.*
*I give you a sapphire stone,*
*for the time and love you spent.'*
*'For untying the strings that held them,*
*when they grew up and left home.*
*I give you this one for courage.'*
*Then the Lord added a garnet stone.*
*'I'll place a stone of amethyst,' He said.*
*'For all the times you spent on your knees,*
*when you asked if I'd take care of your children,*
*and then for having faith in Me.'*
*'I have a pearl for every little sacrifice*

124

## Grief and Loss

*that you made without them knowing.*
*For all the times you went without,*
*to keep them happy, healthy and growing.'*
*'And last of all I have a diamond,*
*the greatest one of all,*
*for sharing unconditional love*
*whether they were big or small.'*
*'It was your love that helped them grow*
*Feeling safe and happy and proud*
*A love so strong and pure*
*It could shift the darkest cloud.'*
*After the Lord placed the last jewel in,*
*He said, 'Your crown is now complete,*
*You've earned your place in Heaven*
*With your children at your feet.'*

## Down the Rabbit Hole and Back Again

Mum's granddaughter Lorna, Philomena's youngest daughter, sang a beautiful melody in her angelic voice called 'Arcady'. Lorna regularly sang for our mum and especially during the final days of Mum's life in the hospital. Lorna's beautiful voice could be heard throughout the hospital ward. Lorna's singing brought tremendous joy to our mum and her smile expressed her comfort and happiness during her final days in our world.

During end-of-life experiences, engaging in activities that bring joy can greatly enhance the emotional wellbeing of both patients and their loved ones. Singing can be a powerful tool for emotional expression, connection and comfort. It has been known to provide solace, reduce stress and uplift spirits.

**Grief and Loss**

## *Arcady lyrics*

I'll go my way a singing down the road to Arcady

The Daffodils are blowing 'neath the scented cherry tree

A merry blackbird's piping, making music as I go

A singing down the valley where the cherry blossoms blow

There's quiet peace in Arcady, and oh, the air is sweet

The flutt'ring cherry petals make a carpet for my feet

And beauty dwells in Arcady while time goes softly by

A selling dreams of gossamer beneath the blue, blue sky

I hear a south wind calling, calling, calling, night and day

It calls me back to Arcady, I can hear it far away

Far across the leafy valley, down the road to Arcady

Calling me, calling me

# Down the Rabbit Hole and Back Again

The lyrics depict a picturesque and idyllic place called Arcady, which is often associated with a paradise or utopia.

In the song, the singer expresses a desire to go to Arcady, a place of tranquillity and beauty. The mention of daffodils, cherry trees and cherry blossoms adds to the imagery of a serene and harmonious environment. The reference to a 'merry blackbird' and the sound of music further enhances the idyllic atmosphere.

The lyrics also convey a sense of longing and nostalgia, as the singer recalls the peacefulness and beauty of Arcady. The south wind calling and beckoning the singer back to Arcady evokes a sense of yearning for a place of happiness and contentment.

# Chapter 16

# Down the Rabbit Hole: Finding Resonance in Alice's Journey

In this final chapter I strive to bring some light humour into my story. As we have heard many times, humour is the best medicine and can help us find a light-hearted perspective even in challenging or surreal experiences.

Certainly, *Alice in Wonderland* is a classic children's novel written by Lewis Carroll. It tells the story of a young girl named Alice who falls down a rabbit hole into a magical and nonsensical world called Wonderland.

## Down the Rabbit Hole and Back Again

For my own once upon a time, in the curious land of childhood, something unexpected happened when I turned eight years old. It was like following the White Rabbit down the rabbit hole, except instead of a whimsical adventure, it led me straight to the hospital. My intuitive little mind had a hunch that there was more to this appendectomy business than met the eye.

Several weeks later as I sat in the backseat, headed to the big hospital in the city, I could not help but feel a strange sense of déjà vu. It was as if I were channelling Alice herself, on the cusp of a grand journey with something big about to be revealed. Like Alice, I was about to embark on an unexpected journey, not fully aware of what lay ahead.

In this outrageous and nonsensical comparison, down the rabbit hole I went into the large and strange place with wide corridors and hospital beds. The adults behaved like Mad Hatters, walking around with their white starched hats, behaving in the most illogical ways, as if they've stumbled upon a tea party hosted by the Mad Hatter himself. Indeed, they must have taken a sip from the Mad Hatter's never-ending teapot of confusion. The adults in the hospital, like the Mad Hatter, had this peculiar expectation that children should not be heard, should not be scared, and definitely should not cry. It seems they have forgotten that hospitals are meant to be places of comfort and care, not a Mad Hatter's tea party with its absurdity.

I may be a child, but I can see the absurdity to it all. I chuckle at the sheer nonsensicality of the situation. Perhaps I should wear my very own giant hat and just play along and inject some fun into the mix.

Later I met the wonderful Cheshire Cat along my journey and loved her mischievous ways having the ability to disappear and reappear at will. Wow, what a gift I thought to myself, I can certainly use these powers to cope with my hospital experiences. And so it was,

## Down the Rabbit Hole: Finding Resonance in Alice's Journey

I was able to tap into Cheshire Cat's magic to disassociate from whatever bad experiences came my way. In this way the Cheshire Cat kept me sane with her big grin and I could only hope that the staff may leave treats out for us.

Finally, I encountered the Queen of Hearts herself, down in Wonderland Ward, wearing a larger Head Sister Nun hat. Perhaps a representation of power and authority. Eyes like hawks to witness from the nursing office window that one innocent kiss on the cheek of a 10-year-old girl. It was sure to send the hospital spiralling into chaos. Hence, the Queen or Nun had a great knack of doling out punishments and I found myself banished to the scorching hot laundry room, ironing bed linen as if my life depended on it. Perhaps I should thank the Queen – I mean, the head nun – for unintentionally giving me a taste of Wonderland's nonsense. Who knew that a hospital could have its own tyrannical ruler? Just like Alice, I found myself caught in a topsy-turvy world where the rules didn't make sense, and punishment was handed out without rhyme or reason.

Regardless, just like Alice, I didn't let the Queen of Hearts – or the head nun – ruin my sense of wonder and joy. I held on to the anticipation of the Christmas season, ready to escape the clutches of this authoritarian figure and reunite with my family. Because, let's face it, nothing is better than Christmas magic to lift your spirits and make you forget about cranky rulers and their irrational punishments.

So, here's to the Queen of Hearts, I mean the head nun, who inadvertently taught me to never take life too seriously and to always find humour in the absurdity of it all. After all, in the grand adventure of life, we're all just a bunch of curious souls trying to navigate through our own Wonderland.

## Down the Rabbit Hole and Back Again

So, my friends, let my story serve as a reminder that even in the most unexpected moments, there is a touch of magic and whimsy waiting to unfold. Trust your gut, follow the White Rabbit, and embrace the journey, for you never know what enchanting surprises lie just beyond the horizon.

# Afterword

As I reflect on writing my story in my words, the process has brought up so many emotions. Some good and some not so good. I am grateful for both.

I have felt as my story has unfolded a shifting, a transformation, that for me would not be possible without writing it down. Stories are told and passed down in many ways, including art, music, movies, writing, yarning, cultural rituals and more.

My story is a deeply personal account of the impact my illness had on our family's life. It is a story I wish to pass down to my own children and grandchildren, so they may understand our family's journey. Through sharing our experiences, I hope to highlight the importance of the bonds that unite us and emphasise the significance of cherishing our loved ones.

In addition, my wish for my book is that those who have lived through a chronic childhood illness, hospitalisation and separation from family, can find solace and healing from reading my story.

There is some kind of nurturing that occurs within the human psyche where sharing an experience with another human seems to help. It's that knowing that someone else knows what I have gone through: and that's enough, as I am not alone.

Resilience is not a destination; it is a lifelong journey. It is a commitment to yourself, a promise to rise each time you fall and seize the opportunity for renewal. It is essential that we actively nurture our resilience by consistently replenishing our inner strength and positivity. This holds true not only for ourselves, but also for our little ones, as we strive to ensure their resilience through continuously refilling their metaphorical buckets.

With heartfelt gratitude,
Breda

# References

Newgrange – World Heritage Site, Ireland's Ancient East https://newgrange.com

Chronic Illness in Children – from Association for the Wellbeing of Children in Healthcare (AWCH) (2008) https://awch.org.au

How the Troubles Began in Northern Ireland (2021) https://www.history.com

Wolesky, Patrick (2023) 'War & Peace in Northern Ireland, The Influence of Music and Musicians During the Troubles'

Robinson, Mary (2008) 'Reflections in Working Towards Peace: Resources for Teachers and Students' https://www.scu.edu

The Aboriginal Heritage Office (2023) https://www.aboriginalheritage.org

## Down the Rabbit Hole and Back Again

Transplant Australia Newsletter (2023) https://www.transplant.org.au

Donaldson, Walter. (1920). Arcady. In Songs of the 1920s, Track 5 [Recorded by Various Artists]. New York, NY: Columbia Records.

Carroll, L. *Alice's Adventures in Wonderland:150*th *Anniversary Edition*, Princeton University Press: Princeton, NJ, (2015)

https://centacare.org.au Making Moments in Playford families (2016).

# About the Author

Breda McAlinden has a background in social work, working for over two decades with disadvantaged individual's families and communities.

Emigrating to Australia from Ireland and living a rich and diverse life, her personal story highlights the importance of family and community in her life. Breda talks about her journey through childhood illness, hospitalisation and separation from her family. Later experiencing renal failure, dialysis, and the triumphant story of receiving her perfect match kidney from her sister Philomena. Breda now fondly refers to her sister Philomena as her 'twin kidney sister'.

Breda has postgraduate education in counselling, life coaching, and teaching mindfulness and meditation.

In later years Breda has worked in creating her private practice, *Holistic Well-being Counselling & Life Coaching,* where she continues to support people with whatever life challenges they are experiencing.


*'Living a life that is purposeful and meaningful gives us passion. and a very good reason for doing what we do best.'*

# Testimonials

'Breda's beautifully written story reminds me of how a wonderful ability to express ourselves in poetry at tough times in our lives brings us real comfort, courage, resilience and great self-leadership skills.

This is a must read for anyone who has visited a dark place and a great reminder than in life there is always light at the end of the *rabbit hole*.'

**—Morgan Pierse**


'A truly heartwarming read; written with such raw emotion and some beautiful poetry and history lessons for added context.

Life can be so wonderful and yet, bloody hard all at the same time. No-one can ever really prepare you for the tough times, so navigating them can be a lonely experience, even when you are surrounded by loving family and friends.

# Down the Rabbit Hole and Back Again

Breda's story certainly reflects this and the coping mechanisms that she established along the way are truly inspiring. It just goes to show that with an abundance of love, faith and support, any hurdles can be overcome.

I loved reading Breda's memoir and I feel privileged to have met Breda in a work capacity and now as a valued friend.'

**—Kerry Prier**

'There is a richness in Breda's memoir; a clear vision of how her life was influenced by the political, cultural, familial and environmental landscapes.

There is a wonderful injection of poetry along Breda's journey. This highlights the power of the written word and how Breda found comfort and peace in writing.

The passing of loved ones, in particular the premature death of Breda's husband; had a profound impact on her life, and the sadness and grief felt is very apparent.

Breda's strength as a child and teenager were shaped by strong family bonds. Such strength continues to guide her to this day; as Breda continues to reflect on life and self-discovery from all the way down the rabbit hole and back again.'

**—Margaret (Mig) Colliar**

# Notes

_____

_____

_____

_____

_____

_____

_____

_____

## Down the Rabbit Hole and Back Again

_____

_____

_____

_____

_____

_____

_____

_____

_____

_____

_____

_____

_____

_____

# Notes